The Handbook

of

Nonsexist Writing

The Handbook
of
Nonsexist
Writing

by

Casey Miller & Kate Swift

Lippincott & Crowell, Publishers·New York

FIRST EDITION
Designed by Ginger Legato

U.S. Library of Congress Cataloging in Publication Data

Miller, Casey.
    The handbook of nonsexist writing.

    Includes bibliographical references and index.
    1. Rhetoric.   2. Sexism in language.   I. Swift, Kate, joint author.   II.
Title.
PB218.M5   808'.02   79-26851
ISBN 0-690-01882-7

---

80 81 82 83 84 10 9 8 7 6 5 4 3 2 1

To the memory of
T'Et and Aunt Kack

Contents

viii CONTENTS

Preface

For whatever reasons—goodwill, a sense of justice, an editor's instructions, the pursuit of clarity—a growing number of writers and speakers are trying to free their language from unconscious semantic bias. This book is intended for them. It will probably be of no use to people who, for an equal number of complex reasons, actively oppose linguistic change or fail to detect the messages of prejudice others hear.

Much of the unconscious bias embedded in modern English stems from cultural attitudes toward women and, to a lesser but significant extent, from cultural expectations damaging to men. Comparable considerations affect members of other groups since standard usage also conceals within it biases based on race, religion, ethnicity, sexual preference, age, and physical handicaps. In focusing on the problems of linguistic sexism, we have tried to make our examples and discussion applicable by analogy to these other human conditions as well.

Many of our examples come from published sources or from radio and television. These are indicated by the use of quotation marks, and the names of public figures, when they occurred, have been retained. When a quotation mentioned the name of someone not widely known, we substituted conventional names like John Doe and Jane Roe out of respect for the person's privacy. Examples not in quotation marks are made up. Personal names occurring in these

1

examples, other than the names of public figures, are also invented and do not represent real people.

We included relevant documentation in a section of reference notes but did not provide the source of every quotation used as an example, although we can attest to their authenticity. The examples are intended to be illustrative only, not sources of factual information. Our aim throughout has been to provide practical suggestions to speakers and writers already committed to equality as well as clarity in style, though in the process we tried to show why an apparently innocuous word or phrase may be injurious.

We are grateful to several friends who read and criticized the manuscript—Virginia Barber, Nancy Henley, James and Ruth Oliver, and Nancy Wilson. We are also especially indebted to Carol Cohen, our editor at Lippincott & Crowell, who not only provided many ideas and examples, but who recognized the need for a book of this kind and invited us to write it.

Casey Miller and Kate Swift

Introduction: Change and Resistance to Change

Every language reflects the prejudices of the society in which it evolved. Since English, through most of its history, evolved in a white, Anglo-Saxon, patriarchal society, no one should be surprised that its vocabulary and grammar frequently reflect attitudes that exclude or demean minorities and women.

But we are surprised. Until recently few people thought much about what English—or any other language for that matter—was saying on a subliminal level. Now that we have begun to look, some startling things have become obvious. What standard English usage says about males, for example, is that they are the species. What it says about females is that they are a subspecies. From these two assertions flow a thousand other enhancing and degrading messages, all encoded in the language we in the English-speaking countries begin to learn almost as soon as we are born.

A sizable number of people would like to do something about these inherited linguistic.biases. But getting rid of them involves more than exposing them and suggesting alternatives. It requires change, and linguistic change is no easier to accept than any other kind. It may even be harder.

At a deep level, changes in a language are threatening because they signal widespread changes in social mores. At a level closer to the surface they are exasperating. We learn certain rules of grammar and usage in school. When

3

they are challenged it is as though we are also being challenged. Our native language is like a second skin, so much a part of us we resist the idea that it is constantly changing, constantly being renewed. Though we know intellectually that the English we speak today and the English of Shakespeare's time are very different, we tend to think of them as the same—static rather than dynamic. "Grammar," a nationally syndicated columnist wrote recently, "is as fixed in its way as geometry."

One of the obstacles to accepting any kind of linguistic change—whether it concerns something as superficial as the pronunciation of *tomato* or as fundamental as sexual bias—is this desire to keep language "pure." In order to see change as natural and inevitable rather than as an affront, we need perspective, and to gain perspective it helps to take a look at some of the changes that have already taken place in English.

To start with, if it were true that "Grammar is as fixed in its way as geometry" we would still, in the twentieth century, be speaking Old English, the earliest version of the tongue we know today: our vocabulary would be almost totally different; we would still be altering a word's form to change the meaning of a sentence instead of shifting words about—as in "Dog bites man," "Man bites dog"— to do the same thing; and we would still have "grammatical" rather than "natural" gender. The last change is important because the gender assigned to nouns and pronouns in Old English, as in most modern European languages, often had no relationship to sex or its absence. The word for "chair," for example, was masculine; the word for "table" was feminine; and the word for "ship" was neuter. In modern English we match gender with sex. That is, we reserve feminine and masculine gender for human beings and other sex-differentiated animals or, in flights of fancy, for nonliving things (like ships) onto which we project human associations. At least theoretically all other English nouns and pronouns are neuter or, in the case of agent-nouns like *teacher* and *president,* sex-neutral.

Greatly as these grammatical simplifications invigorated

English, some of its special richness comes from the flexibility of its vocabulary. The English lexicon is a kind of uninhibited conglomeration put together over the centuries from related Indo-European languages and, though far less frequently, from languages as unrelated to English as Chinese, Nahuatl, and Yoruba.

Yet despite the hospitality of English to outside as well as internal influences, many people, including many language experts, become upset when confronted with new words or grammatical modifications they happen not to like. H. W. Fowler, whose widely used *Dictionary of Modern English Usage* was first published in 1926, deplored such "improperly formed" words as *amoral, bureaucrat, speedometer, pacifist,* and *coastal,* terms so commonly used today we take them for granted. His scorn for *electrocute* (formed by analogy to *execute*) pushed him beyond compassion or reason. The word, he wrote, "jars the unhappy latinist's nerves much more cruelly than the operation denoted jars those of its victims" (an emotional excess Sir Ernest Gowers, editor of the current edition of Fowler, mercifully deleted).

Lexicographers are less judgmental. In compiling dictionaries, they try to include as many commonly used words as space allows, whether the words are "properly formed" or not. Dictionaries, however, cannot help but lag behind actual use, and so they are not always reliable indicators of new or altered meanings. The 1977 edition of one college dictionary defines *youth* as (among other things) ". . . the part of life between childhood and manhood" and "A young person, especially a young man," and some people continue to use the word in both those limited senses. When film director Martha Coolidge approached a Hollywood producer about making a "low-budget youth picture," he is reported to have said, "No gays or women; it's a male subject." Actually the accepted meaning of *youth* is shifting faster than the producer realized or dictionaries can keep up with. Under the headline "Stolen Horse Is Found by Relentless Searcher," a news story in the *New York Times* twice referred to the horse's owner, a sixteen-year-old girl, as a youth: "After Rocky was stolen . . . the youth called every stable and horse handler she could find" and "the youth's parents brought a trailer . . . for the trip home." Though the term may once have been anomalous when used of a young woman, today it is a recognized common-gender noun, and the next round of dictionaries will no doubt add their authority to the change.

Changes in usage often occur slowly and imperceptibly, but some take place with dramatic speed, seemingly overnight. Such was the case in the 1960s when *black* replaced *Negro.* How the change occurred and something of the power of words was described by Congresswoman Shirley Chisholm:

> A few short years ago, if you called most Negroes "blacks," it was tantamount to calling us niggers. But now black is beautiful, and black is proud. There are relatively few people, white or black, who do not recognize what has happened. Black people have freed themselves from the dead weight of albatross blackness that once hung around their necks. They have done it by picking it up in their arms and holding it out with pride for all the world to see. . . . [A]nd they have found that the skin that was once seen as symbolizing their chains is in reality their badge of honor.

Although some people are still reluctant to accept this use of *black,* the balance has clearly shifted in its favor, and the familiar alternatives *Negro, colored,* and *Afro-American* are heard less often.

Ironically, those who deal with words professionally or avocationally can be the most resistant to linguistic changes. Like Fowler, they may know so much about etymology that any deviation from the classical pattern of word formation grates on their ears. Or having accepted certain rules of grammar as correct, they may find it impossible to acknowledge that those particular rules could ever be superseded.

What many people find hardest to accept is that a word which used to mean one thing now means another, and that continuing to use it in its former sense—no matter how impeccable its etymological credentials—can only invite misunderstanding. When the shift in meaning happened centuries ago, no problem lingers. One may be fully aware that *girl* once meant "a young person of either sex" and yet not feel compelled to invite misunderstanding by referring to a sexually mixed group of children as girls. When the change happens in one's lifetime, recognition and acceptance may be harder.

The word *intriguing* is such a case. Once understood to mean "conniving" or "deceitful" (like the verb *intrigue*, it comes—through the French *intriguer*, "to puzzle"—from the Latin *intricare*, "to entangle"), *intriguing* now means "engaging the interest to a marked degree," as Webster's Third New International Dictionary noted some two decades ago. People still make statements like "They are an intriguing pair" with the intention of issuing a warning, but chances are the meaning conveyed is "They are a fascinating pair," because that is how a new generation of writers and speakers understands and uses the word. In one sense precision has been lost; in another it has only shifted. Today no one expects a 6-horsepower boat to be pulled by six horses.

The transformation of *man* over the past thousand years may be the most troublesome and significant change ever to overtake an English word. Once a synonym for "human being," *man* has gradually narrowed in meaning to become a synonym for "adult male human being" only. Put simply in the words of a popular dictionary for children, "A boy grows up to be a man. Father and Uncle George are both men." These are the meanings of *man* and *men* native speakers of English internalize because they are the meanings which from infancy on we hear applied in everyday speech. Though we may later acquire the information that *man* has another, "generic" meaning, we do not accept it with the same certainty we accept the children's dictionary definition and its counterparts: A girl does not grow up to be a man. Mother and Aunt Teresa are not men; they are women.

To go on using in its former sense a word whose meaning has changed is counterproductive. The point is not that we should recognize semantic change, but that in order to be precise, in order to be understood, we must. The difference is a fundamental one in any discussion of linguistic bias, for some writers think their freedom of expression and artistic integrity are being compromised when they are asked to avoid certain words or grammatical forms. Is it ever justifiable, for example, for publishers to expect their authors to stop using the words *forefathers, man,* and *he* as though they were sex-inclusive? Is this not unwarranted interference with an author's style? Even censorship?

The public counts on those who disseminate factual information—especially on people in the mass media and the publishers of textbooks and other forms of nonfiction— to be certain that what they tell us is as accurate as research and the conscientious use of language can make it. Only recently have we become aware that conventional English usage, including the generic use of masculine-gender words, often obscures the actions, the contributions, and sometimes the very presence of women. Turning our backs on that insight is an option, of course, but it is an option like teaching children the world is flat. In this respect, continuing to use English in ways that have become misleading is no different from misusing data, whether the misuse is inadvertent or planned.

The need today, as always, is to be in command of language, not used by it, and so the challenge is to find clear, convincing, graceful ways to say accurately what we want to say. That is what this book attempts to do, and it begins, appropriately, with more about *man.*

1 | *Man* as a False Generic

"Development of the Uterus in Rats, Guinea Pigs,
and Men"

Generic terms, like *rats* and *guinea pigs*, are equally applicable to a class or group and to its individual members. Terms used of a class or group that are not applicable to all its members are false generics. The reason the research-report title quoted above sounds incongruous is that *men* in that context is a false generic. This was not always so.

HISTORICAL BACKGROUND

Ercongota, the daughter of a seventh-century English king, is described in *The Anglo-Saxon Chronicle* as "a wonderful man." In Old English the word *man* meant "person" or "human being," and when used of an individual was equally applicable to either sex. It was parallel to the Latin *homo*, "a member of the human species," not *vir*, "an adult male of the species." English at the time of Ercongota had separate words to distinguish the sexes: *wer* (equivalent to the Latin *vir*) meant "adult male," and *wif* meant "adult female." The combined forms *waepman* and *wifman* meant, respectively, "adult male person" and "adult female person."

In the course of time *wifman* evolved into the modern

9

word *woman,* and *wif* narrowed in meaning to become *wife* as we use that word today. *Man* eventually ceased to be used of individual women and replaced *wer* and *waepman* as a specific term distinguishing an adult male from an adult female. But *man* continued to be used in generalizations about both sexes. As long as most generalizations about people were made by men about men, the ambiguity nestling in this dual usage was either not noticed or thought not to matter.

By the eighteenth century the modern, narrow sense of *man* was firmly established as the predominant one. When Edmund Burke, writing of the French Revolution, used *men* in the old, inclusive way, he took pains to spell out his meaning: "Such a deplorable havoc is made in the minds of men (both sexes) in France . . ." Thomas Jefferson did not make the same distinction in declaring that "all men are created equal" and "governments are instituted among men, deriving their just powers from the consent of the governed." In a time when women, having no vote, could neither give nor withhold consent, Jefferson had to be using the word *men* in its principal sense of "males," and it probably never occurred to him that anyone would think otherwise.

Current dictionaries still define *man* in both its narrow and broad senses. In the New College Edition of the American Heritage Dictionary (1978), for example, the definition is "1. An adult male human being, as distinguished from a female. 2. Any human being, regardless of sex or age; a member of the human race; a person. 3. The human race; mankind. . . ." The point at issue, therefore, is whether parts 2 and 3 of that definition are still fully operative or whether the first and exclusive meaning has, in effect, become the only valid one.

Recent studies of college students and school children indicate that the broad definitions of *man* and *men,* although still taught, have to a significant degree become inoperative at a subliminal level. Phrases like *economic man* and *political man,* or statements like "Man domesticated animals" and "Man is a dreamer," it turns out, tend to call up images of male people only, not female people or females and males together.

Lexicographers appear to agree. Although they do not label the supposedly generic meaning of *man* obsolete, they write some definitions as though we all know it is. For example, Webster's New Collegiate Dictionary (1979) defines a man-about-town as "a worldly and socially active man." But if *man* sometimes means "any human being," should not the definition of *man-about-town* read "a worldly and socially active person of the male sex"? How can the definers be sure we will know without being told that a man-about-town is never a woman?

Lexicographers are aware, of course, that ever since English lost a specifically male-gender counterpart to *woman,* *man* has been shifting away from generality toward specificity. They also know that the limited meaning of *man* is the only one native speakers of English internalize as applying to an individual. Thus when Diana Nyad swam from Bimini to the Florida coast in 1979 the news media did not report that

> Marathon swimmer Diana Nyad became the first man to swim the 60 miles from the Bahamas to Florida.

They said, with incidental variations,

> "Marathon swimmer Diana Nyad became the first person to swim . . ."

What lexicographers and grammarians are less attuned to, however, is the extent to which this narrowing is felt. Because gender in modern English corresponds to sex or its absence, native speakers of the language increasingly sense the same contradiction in calling women "men" that they would feel in calling girls "boys" or daughters "sons." In reporting the remark of a member of Congress,

> " 'Every man on this subcommittee is for public works,' "

the *Wall Street Journal* appended a comment:

> "There are two women on the subcommittee, and they are for public works, too."

Writers who persist in using *man* in its old sense often slip unconsciously from the general meaning to the limited one. The switch, unfortunately, is rarely discernible to their readers, who have no way of telling that generalizations about human beings have become generalizations about males. Yet we know it does happen—if not how often—because every once in a while an author's unconscious lapse shows through, as in this example from a book review:

> "[T]he book can be read with interest by people who . . . wonder about strange facts: why men speak and animals don't, why man feels so sad in the 20th century, why war is man's greatest pleasure."

Readers who assume "men speak" and "man feels so sad" refer to all of us are brought up short by the final phrase. Whether war is the greatest pleasure of most men is debatable, but would anyone assert that it is the greatest pleasure of women?

Other lapses are even more revealing. One author, ostensibly generalizing about all human beings, wrote:

> "As for man, he is no different from the rest. His back aches, he ruptures easily, his women have difficulties in childbirth. . . ."

If *man* and *he* were truly generic, the parallel phrase would have been

> he has difficulties in childbirth.

And in a magazine article on aggression, where the context also indicated *man* was supposed to include women, readers were startled to come upon the statement

> "[M]an can do several things which the animal cannot do. . . . Eventually, his vital interests are not only life, food, access to females, etc., but also values, symbols, institutions. . . ."

In each case the present meaning of *man* had asserted itself, leading the writer to equate the species with its male members.

As we know from modern psychology, man overlooks what he does not want to see—and so does woman. But males may have a greater vested interest in preserving the way things were than in acknowledging the way they are. If the word *man* were not so emotionally charged and politically useful, its ambiguity would have led long ago to its disuse in any but the limited sense it immediately brings to mind. So the question for writers and speakers becomes, how can we get along without *man* in the old sense, that archaic crutch we no longer need but to which we have become habituated?

Alternatives to "Generic" *Man*

In Clichés

Compare the sentence

> When a shave and a haircut cost two bits, even the man in the street patronized a barber

with the sentence

> Though Mary Ferrara is already well known in the consumer advocacy movement, she'll need the support of the man in the street if she runs for office.

In the first, "the man in the street" clearly refers to males. In the second, the phrase is ambiguous. Perhaps the writer knows that Mary Ferrara already has a large following of women but needs the support of men. But does the reader know it? Phrases like *the common man* or *the average man* would have been equally unclear. Assuming the candidate needs the support of both women and men, the sentence could read:

> . . . she'll need a broad power base (*or* the support of ordinary voters *or* of the average voter) if she runs for office.

Another pair of sentences illustrates the lack of clarity in a cliché like *the working man:*

> The rich cannot possibly appreciate the impact of inflation on the average working man.

> The average working man earns almost twice as much as the average working woman.

The second example says what it means; one has no way of knowing whether the author of the first had males only in mind or was using English loosely. In either case, the sentence reveals careless thinking that would have been corrected if the writer had not used a false generic:

> The rich cannot possibly appreciate the impact of inflation on the average wage earner (*or* the average worker).

Generalizations about people couched in terms like "a man who," "if a man," or "no man" are clearer when rephrased to include people of both sexes (unless, of course, only males are intended). For instance,

> A man who lies constantly needs a good memory

is made more realistic when "a man" is replaced by *someone* or *anyone*. Or better still:

> A chronic liar needs a good memory.

Similar phrases like

> If a man can drive 500 miles in ten hours . . .

> No man would be safe from nuclear fallout if . . .

can be recast in a variety of ways, for example:

> If someone (*or* If you *or* If one *or* If Jones) can drive . . .

or

> If it is possible to drive . . .

> No one (*or* No human being) would be safe from nuclear fallout if . . .

Terms for the Human Species

" . . . it is now thought that a million years ago and more, earth was populated with more or less manlike creatures, descended not from apes but from some forefather of both apes and men."

"The personal commitment of a man to his skill, the intellectual commitment and the emotional commitment working together as one, has made the Ascent of Man."

"Man has learned a lot. He has invented ever so many things. Someday you may even be able to go and visit the other planets."

Because scientists have traditionally "translated" the Latin term *Homo sapiens* as "man" rather than "human being," resistance to giving up this once-generic term is particularly strong in the scientific community. Those who write about anthropology and the biological sciences, including the authors of children's books on these subjects, are frequently addicted to using *man* in contexts like the above. From *near-man* through *early man* to *true man* and *modern man*, accounts of human evolution are couched in terms of *mankind* and *forefathers*, with frequent references to "his" cultural artifacts, the effect of erect posture in enabling "him" to see farther, "his" animals, crops, pottery, villages, etc., etc.

An entirely different image is projected in a story headlined "New Clues to Ancient Life" published in the newsletter *Indian Affairs*. Reporting on archaeological findings at the Koster site in Illinois, the writer, instead of relying on *man*, used terms like "people" and "ancient people," "residents of the ancient village," "the site's inhabitants," and "these early human populations." The newsletter is a model of nonbiased writing, and its commitment is evidently shared by the leader of the Koster exploration, archaeologist Stuart Struever, who is quoted in the article:

"If we are to measure 'cultural success' in part by the ability of a human population to establish an equilibrium with its environment that can be sustained over the long haul, then these Koster residents were successful people, indeed."

Used in broad, sweeping generalizations, *man* frequently—perhaps usually—conveys misinformation.

When ancient man developed agriculture . . .

rejects, as far as a listener or reader has any way of knowing, the extensive evidence now available indicating that women were the earliest cultivators of plants.

Men have always hoped to conquer disease

not only appears to disregard women's interest in ending illness but also to ignore the important advances toward that goal made by women—from the anonymous healers and discoverers of curative plants to Nobel laureates. Authenticity is better served by phrases like

When our ancestors (*or* people *or* human beings *or* our forebears) first developed agriculture . . .

Human societies (*or* Men and women *or* Women and men) have always hoped to conquer disease.

Sometimes the best solution is to rephrase a thought completely:

The conquest of disease has always been a goal of human societies.

The historian Mary Beard pointed out many years ago that most historians use *man* in ways that obscure women's contributions to civilization; unfortunately they, and others, continue to do so. The list of books with titles like *The Condition of Man, The Identity of Man, Man's Unconquerable Mind, The Family of Man, Man and the Universe, The Tree Where Man Was Born,* and *Mars and the Mind of Man,* appears to be endless. The popular writer Peter Farb, an anthropologist and linguist who once wrote a book called *Man's Rise to Civilization as Shown by the Indians of North America,* has apparently had second thoughts about what such titles imply. He calls a more recent book *Humankind.*

Men of Letters and Other Women

> "The history of every country begins in the heart of a man or a woman."

Willa Cather expressed that conviction at the end of a moving passage in *O Pioneers!* As a woman writing about a woman, she was not likely to fall into the trap set by the false generic *man.* A noted sculptor was less in tune with reality when he said:

> "A work of art is beautiful because a man did it."

One assumes he did not mean to exclude a sculpture by Louise Nevelson or a painting by Georgia O'Keeffe, yet his choice of words betrayed him into doing so. Though one can only guess, it may be his meaning was something like

> A work of art is beautiful because a human being created it.

Unintentional exclusion is hard to distinguish from intentional exclusion. Did a book reviewer who described George Will as

> "the principal public philosopher and man of letters of our generation"

mean to exclude, let us say, Susan Sontag? If he had called Will

> the principal public philosopher and writer of our generation

that particular question would not have come up.

Women in art, in science, in education, and in business and politics are adding a dimension to the human environment that was previously lacking. As Hanna Holborn Gray, now president of the University of Chicago, said in a baccalaureate address at Yale:

> "The institution of the university is not, in Emerson's phrase, the lengthened shadow of one man, but rather that of many men and women who care for its purposes."

If Gray had said

> The institution of the university is not, in Emerson's phrase, the lengthened shadow of one man, but rather of many men who care for its purposes

she would have conveyed a different message, even if in her own mind she intended the word *men* to be understood inclusively.

Man as a Verb

The verb *to man* comes from the noun and dates from the Middle English period when it was used in the sense of furnishing a ship or fort or castle with men to operate or defend it. By analogy *man* came to be used in the sense of "to work at," as in "to man" a production line or information booth (though seldom, if ever, a tea table). *Work, staff, serve at (on), operate,* and other alternatives can be used instead of *man:*

They had to man the pumps all night.	They had to work the pumps all night.
We asked the Girl Scouts to man the exhibit.	We asked the Girl Scouts to run the exhibit.
The emergency room must be manned at all times.	The emergency room must be staffed (*or* covered) at all times.
Man the barricades!	Mount the barricades!

Man's Inhumanity to Men

If males often get sole credit for great human accomplishments attributed to *man,* they also often get sole blame for history's horrors. Whether the writers quoted below were visualizing males only, or females and males, is anybody's guess—though it need not have been, as the rewritten versions show:

" . . . why should [visitors from space] not see the same virtues in domesticating human beings that men realized long ago when they domesticated cattle, horses, dogs and cats? Or impressed other human beings into slavery?"

. . . why should [visitors from space] not see the same virtues in domesticating human beings that humans themselves realized long ago when they domesticated cattle, horses, dogs and cats? Or impressed other human beings (*or* their fellow humans) into slavery?

"Muir knew that man's spirit can only survive in a land that is spacious and unpolluted. . . . He felt that man should come as a visitor to these places—the mountains, river canyons, coasts, deserts and swamps—to learn, not to leave his mark."

Muir knew that the human spirit can only survive in a land that is spacious and unpolluted. . . . He felt that we should come as visitors to these places . . . to learn, not to leave our mark.

"Man should be presented [to children] as a steward of the animals rather than the 'most intelligent' creature who has the right to do as he pleases with the other animals."

People should be presented [to children] as stewards of the animals rather than the 'most intelligent' of creatures with the right to do as we please with the other animals.

"[Hart] Crane seems to have believed that daily life enforced a sufficient degree of penance and that a man had the right to make the best of it, taking his pleasures where he found them."

Crane seems to have believed that daily life enforced a sufficient degree of penance and that we all have the right to make the best of it, taking our pleasures where we find them.

Anyone who chooses to use *man* in its old, generic sense has centuries of precedent behind their choice. But even centuries of precedent crumble if those on the receiving end hear a different meaning from the one intended. When

Edith Bunker, on the television series "All in the Family," quoted Sam Walter Foss's

"Let me live in my house by the side of the road
And be a friend of man,"

Archie's response was,

"Yeah, I heard about them kind of houses in the Army."

Man in Compounds

"America's manpower begins with boy power"

"The annual exhibit of the Connecticut Society of Craftsmen—which includes women artists as well—opens Thursday. . . ."

The exclusion and ambiguity characteristic of *man* when it is used generically extend to compound words like *manpower* and *craftsman.* Before discussing such words, however, it is important to note that *woman* and *human* are not, as is often implied, compounds incorporating the modern word *man. Woman* is a combination of *wif,* meaning "an adult female," and *man* in its lost sense of "a human being irrespective of sex or age." *Human* is from the Latin *humanus,* akin to *homo,* also meaning "human being." Neither has any more relation to a word originally meaning "male person" than do words like *manager, manufacture, manuscript,* and *manipulate,* which come from the Latin *manus,* "hand." The most that can be said about the belabored form of ridicule which suggests we must find alternatives for every word containing the syllable *man* is that *wobody, huperson, personipulate,* etc., are ideas whose time has gone.

Man as a Prefix

"Should all despair that have revolted wives, the tenth of mankind would hang themselves." —William Shakespeare

"The infinite simplicity and silliness of mankind and womankind . . ."   —Anthony Trollope

"When I speak of mankind, one thing I *don't* mean is womankind."   —Man in a Steig cartoon

For more than four centuries *mankind* has been used, as
in the examples above, to differentiate men from women.
To avoid ambiguity and occasional ineptness, as in

> The Pap test, which has greatly reduced mortality from
> uterine cancer, is a boon to mankind,

alternative terms that clearly designate people as distinguished from other forms of life can be useful:

> The Pap test, which has greatly reduced mortality from
> uterine cancer, is a boon to humanity (*or* humankind).

An even more serious drawback to *mankind* when used
to mean people collectively is that, willy-nilly, like *man,* it
imposes the image of maleness on the entire species.
Which in turn often fosters an androcentric view of the
rest of nature.

> "Will mankind murder Mother Earth or will he redeem
> her?"

asks a historian. The effect of the question may be less
dramatic when the imagery of male aggressor and female
victim is removed, but since such stereotypical behavior
has failed to benefit humanity in the past, rewording the
question might suggest at least part of the answer:

> Will human beings destroy the earth's life-sustaining envi-
> ronment or will they redeem it?

Speakers and writers often use *man*-prefixed compounds
in contexts where *man* represents males alone or both
males and females, but they tend to avoid such compounds
as incongruous when the subjects are explicitly female.

> The only water supply is a manmade pond, which the villag-
> ers created by damming a small stream

conveys an assumption of male involvement. If the writer
knew the dam had been built entirely by women, the sentence might have read:

The only water supply is an artificial pond, which the women of the village created by damming a small stream.

When explaining whether something has been made by women, men, or both is irrelevant—and it usually is—various sex-neutral alternatives to *manmade* are available, including *handmade, hand-built, synthetic, manufactured, fabricated, machine-made,* and *constructed:*

The cave appears to be natural, but it was completely excavated by hand (*or* built by hand *or* hand-built).

All materials in these shoes are synthetic (*or* manufactured).

Since the showcase is only two feet deep, the illusion of great depth is simulated (*or* cleverly created).

Another solution is to omit the adjective entirely. Using an earlier example:

The only water supply is a pond the villagers created by damming a small stream.

When Bryan Allen pedaled his way across the English Channel in the *Gossamer Albatross,* most news reports used the term "manpowered flight." Possibly with the thought that a future air cyclist will be a woman, Doug Tunnell referred on CBS News to

"The first human-powered flight across the Channel"

and *Time* magazine came up with

"muscle-powered flight."

In some contexts a compound like *manpower* clearly excludes females, as in the slogan "America's manpower begins with boy power." On the other hand, an employment agency called Manpower® Temporary Services contracts for per diem secretaries and typists, most of whom are women, and a similar agency advertises one of its divisions as "Kelly Girl®—Male and Female—ALL OFFICE SKILLS." Outside the world of registered trademarks like these, *girl* need not be stretched to include boy (or man), and *man-*

power is usually replaceable with *personnel, staff, work force, available workers,* or *human resources,* as in:

With the signing of the new contracts our manpower needs will double.	With the signing of the new contracts our personnel needs will double.
"Although the FDA hasn't yet formally responded to the petition, agency officials say they don't have enough manpower to give the noodle issue a high priority."	. . . agency officials say they don't have enough staff to give the noodle issue a high priority.
The development of alternative forms of energy requires both technology and manpower.	The development of alternative forms of energy requires both technology and human resources.
"A study of nursing manpower is in progress."	A study of available nurses (or the nursing work force) is in progress.

It is worth noting in this connection that the former Manpower Administration of the United States Department of Labor has been renamed. The new name, which better characterizes the organization's function, is the Employment and Training Administration.

Man-hour is an imprecise term at best, especially when one man's hour may be another man's or woman's forty-five minutes. If a unit of work is measured according to the time the average worker takes to do it, why not call it a *work-hour?* Or the name of the job may suggest another alternative:

Direct dialing saved the telephone company millions of man-hours.	Direct dialing saved the telephone company millions of operator-hours.

Manhole cover is one of the terms people like to caricature by suggesting *personhole cover* as the alternative. Since the holes that provide access to sewers, water mains, conduits, boilers, and the like are utility holes, it seems reasonable to call their covers either *access covers* or *utility-hole covers,* as in

> The explosion blew a utility-hole cover ten feet into the air.

> The boiler's access cover, which is usually bolted in place, had been removed.

Man as a Suffix

A few usage critics maintain that compounds ending in unaccented *man* are always sex-neutral: *layman, tradesman, townsman.* (At least one linguist has suggested, perhaps facetiously, that generic interpretation of these words can best be assured by spelling them as they are pronounced, m-u-n.) More often, however, arbiters of usage assign generic status in some instances and not in others—and their reasons are usually hard to discern.

Spokesman, for example, is considered sex-inclusive by the *New York Times,* whose *Manual of Style and Usage* (1976) forbids either *spokeswoman* or *spokesperson.* Yet the paper does permit its writers to use *saleswoman,* which may be an indication that whoever makes such decisions thinks *salesman* applies to males only. Why anyone should decide it is all right for women to be called "saleswomen" but not "spokeswomen" is unclear. Not only have both terms been in use for some three hundred years, but the earliest citation for *spokeswoman* provided by the Oxford English Dictionary is dated 1654, fifty years before the dictionary's first citation for *saleswoman.*

In the absence of a logical basis for such decisions, even the *New York Times* has trouble keeping the troops in line, as was evident from a recent *Times* story that noted:

> "A hospital spokesperson said Doe's injuries were 'nothing too critical.' "

To eliminate such insubordination, the *Times* might adopt the alternatives offered by the *Associated Press Stylebook,* which approves both *spokeswoman* and *spokesman* (depending on the person's sex),

> A hospital spokeswoman said Doe's injuries were "nothing too critical,"

and suggests, if the sex of the individual is not known, that writers use *representative*.

> A representative of the corporation will meet with the press at 4 P.M.

The *Man* in the Chair

For some reason, what to call the person who heads an academic department or chairs a committee or meeting arouses great anxiety. *Chairman,* according to the *New York Times* style manual, "suffices for both sexes," and so the *Times* does not allow either *chairwoman* or *chairperson.* The National Association of Parliamentarians takes the same position, as does a newly revised edition of *Robert's Rules of Order.* However, others disagree, and for good reasons.

According to the Oxford English Dictionary, *chairman* has been used since at least 1654 and *chairwoman* since 1699. In each of the seventeenth-century quotations the dictionary provides to illustrate the use of *chairman,* the person referred to was clearly male, and none of the citations from later periods shows the use of this word for a female. On the contrary, words like *gentlewoman, countrywoman, laywoman,* and *stateswoman* were recognized counterparts to *gentleman, countryman, layman,* and *statesman;* and women who worked as cleaners and launderers were called *charwomen, washerwomen,* and *scrubwomen,* not *charmen, washermen,* or *scrubmen.*

Since the current aversion to using *woman* in compounds like *chairwoman* and *spokeswoman* cannot be attributed to lack of precedent, is there some other explanation? Perhaps *chairwoman* sounds less important and *spokeswoman* less authoritative than their masculine-gender counterparts. This could explain why some women who achieve positions of leadership still call themselves "chairmen," a term already invested with prestige and power by generations of male incumbents. Or could it be that at least some women go along with the unconscious desire of some men to keep terms like *chairman, alderman,* and *congressman* "official," thereby guarding a traditional male bailiwick from outsiders?

Whatever the reasons for its disfavor, *chairwoman* is a historically sound parallel to *chairman,* and it pays a woman the courtesy of recognizing both her sex and her achievement. It does not, however, solve the problem of what to use as an indefinite, sex-inclusive title. In addition to the much maligned but persistent *chairperson,* the term *chairer* has emerged, and some groups and institutions have chosen to use entirely different titles like *presider, coordinator, president,* and *convener.*

A more obvious solution is provided by the word *chair,* which many national organizations and university departments have already adopted:

> The new chair will take office at the annual meeting in May.

> Witherspoon has been named chair of the English Department.

> John Smith, Chair, Finance Committee

The lexicographer Alma Graham points out that *chair* has been recognized, in the sense of "the occupant of the chair . . . as invested with its dignity," since the seventeenth century, just as *the Crown* has been used for the monarch, or *the Oval Office* has come to stand for the President of the United States. "Address your remarks to the chair" illustrates metonymy, a figure of speech in which something is called by the name of something else associated with it. Few people would understand an injunction to "address the chair" as an order to talk to a piece of furniture.

People as *Men*

Italians, Russians, Iranians, Pakistanis, Australians, and *Japanese,* to pick some random examples, can refer to either females or males. In contrast, terms like *Englishmen, Frenchmen,* and *Irishmen* are ambiguous if used nonspecifically.

> Englishmen are said to prefer tea to coffee

presumably means

> The English are said to prefer tea to coffee

whereas

> Englishmen are said to prefer blonds

is probably intended to refer to the preferences of males.

Precedent for terms like *laywoman* and *stateswoman* as counterparts to *layman* and *statesman* is well documented, as already mentioned (see page 25). Plural forms, when the group specified includes both sexes, may be somewhat more recalcitrant, but they yield, and in the process ambiguity is avoided:

"Obviously few laymen are knowledgeable enough to effectively judge the qualifications of an anesthesiologist."	Obviously few lay people are knowledgeable enough . . . *or* Obviously special training is needed to effectively judge the qualifications of an anesthesiologist.
The show includes the work of craftsmen from every state.	The show includes the work of craftspeople (*or* artisans) from every state.

(See also **Fellow,** page 108, for a discussion of *fellowman.*)

Public *Man*servants

Congressman, assemblyman, councilman, selectman, etc., originated as masculine-gender designations when women's participation in the councils of government was, with rare exceptions like a queen's, unheard of, even unthinkable. In the words of Thomas Jefferson,

> Were our State a pure democracy, in which all its inhabitants should meet together to transact all their business,

there would yet be excluded from their deliberations, 1, infants, until arrived at years of discretion. 2. Women, who, to prevent depravation of morals and ambiguity of issue, could not mix promiscuously in the public meetings of men. 3. Slaves, from whom the unfortunate state of things with us takes away the right of will and of property.

Now that women's participation in government on an equal basis with men is no longer unthinkable, the use of new terms like *congresswoman, assemblywoman, councilwoman,* and *selectwoman* shows that the older titles were not sex-neutral, and that they remain designations appropriate only for males.

New sex-inclusive language is emerging, however. Present alternatives to the false generic *congressman* include *member of Congress* and *representative,* and no doubt other ways will also evolve to designate those elected to offices which were once male domains. A member of a council, city or otherwise, is a *councillor,* for example. In line with the ancient linguistic process whereby adjectives are converted into nouns, a member of Congress may someday be simply a *congressional,* just as a member of a nation is a *national.*

Job Titles

Like the titles of public offices, most job titles ending in *man* date from a time when only males performed the jobs described. It was natural to speak of an *insurance man, delivery man, draftsman,* or *newsboy* because, with the possible exception of *businessman,* the masculine-gender terms matched the sex of nearly everyone doing the jobs described.

Not so today: girls have newspaper delivery routes and women sell insurance, deliver packages, draft structural plans, and run successful businesses, making the old job titles, when retained, discriminatory. If a job category is labeled *lineman* or *repairman,* for instance, whoever does the hiring may look on the job as unsuitable for a woman. Furthermore, employers who use sex-differentiating titles like *salesman* and *saleswoman,* or *forelady* and *foreman,* often adopt two separate pay scales for the same work and pay their male employees more. Although to comply with the law some employers carefully advertise a position as being open to both sexes, they keep the old sex-labeled titles. These act as a code, psychologically inhibiting women from applying for such jobs as *kennelman, stockman,* or *busboy,* and men from applying for jobs with titles ending in *woman, lady,* or *-ess.*

Similarly, job titles like *hat-check girl* and *junior executive,* which imply that youth is a prerequisite for the job, encourage age discrimination on the part of employers and can deter older people from applying.

In response to such considerations, the United States Department of Labor began in the early 1970s to revise its occupational classification system. In 1975 the department published *Job Title Revisions to Eliminate Sex- and Age-Referent Language from the Dictionary of Occupational Titles, Third Edition,* a book of some 400 pages available at many public libraries. Also in recognition of the serious impact of occupational terminology, the District of Columbia and a growing number of states, including California, Georgia, Minnesota, Montana, New York, and Wyoming, have officially changed the term *workmen's compensation* to *workers' compensation.* Some of the Department of Labor's job-title changes are:

From	To
advertising layout man	advertising layout planner
airline steward, stewardess	flight attendant
cameraman, camera girl	camera operator
charwoman	charworker
draftsman	drafter
fisherman	fisher
forelady, foreman	supervisor
gateman	gate tender
hat-check girl	hat-check attendant
junior executive	executive trainee
laundress, laundryman	laundry worker
lineman	line installer, line repairer

longshoreman	stevedore
maid	house worker
office boy, girl	office helper
pressman	press operator
repairman	repairer
salesman	sales agent, sales associate
seamstress	sewer, mender
signalman	signaller
watchman	guard

There are other alternatives, of course, for anyone not limited to the titles used in official job descriptions, and speakers and writers often need variety to avoid monotonous repetition. *Worker* is a useful suffix, as in *longshoreworker* for *longshoreman.* That particular term is a shortening of "along shore," making *worker* a logical addition, and since no one thinks titles like *garmentworker, steelworker,* and *pieceworker* sound funny, why should *longshoreworker?* Resistance to such terms as *repairer* (for *repairman*) and *launderer* (for *laundress* and *laundryman*) is also odd considering the frequency of *-er* and *-or* endings in other agent-nouns: *explorer, bookkeeper, helper, lawyer, painter, photographer, laborer, auditor, conductor,* etc.

With some compounds ending in *man* the solution of simply dropping the last syllable revives a former usage that proves to be still serviceable. *Watchman,* for instance, can become *watch,* used from the sixteenth to the nineteenth centuries to mean "one who watches . . . for the purposes of guarding and protecting life and property."

Alternatives to *salesman, saleswoman,* and their plurals are numerous, including the long-accepted *salesperson:*

Ask any salesperson for help if you don't find what you need.

Our sales people (*or* agents *or* brokers) have a weekly conference.

He was a sales representative for IBM before coming here.

The sales force (*or* sales staff) is being reorganized.

We'll need more salesclerks for the Christmas season.

Anyone who adamantly refuses to use *person* as a suffix (see **Person,** page 117) probably has to settle, when speaking of a jury, for the parallel terms *foreman* and *forewoman,* but the person in charge of workers in a factory or on a construction job can be a *boss, job boss,* or *supervisor.*

Weatherman, newsman, anchorman, and similar designations in which the *man* ending is clearly accented have never been considered sex-inclusive, and women in these posts are usually assigned other job titles. During the 1950s, women who replaced men as television weather reporters were called "weather girls" (although their predecessors had not been called "weather boys"). The common-gender *weather people* may evoke shades of the Weather Underground for some, but there are other possibilities:

> Channel 5 hired a new weathercaster last month.
>
> A weather reporter's popularity rating is likely to go up and down with the weather,

or, where the title describes the trained specialist,

> The article was written by a meteorologist on the staff of the National Weather Service.

Newsman and *anchorman* are easily made sex-inclusive:

> You are invited to send a reporter (*or* news representative *or* newscaster) to the launching.
>
> The Journalist of the Year Award will be announced next Tuesday.
>
> Who will get the job of anchor on the six o'clock news?

Although many common-gender job titles have been readily accepted and are being used routinely, others are resisted by people in the occupations specified. For example, some individuals and organizations in the fishing industry, including some women, objected when the National Marine Fisheries Service began to use *fisher* instead of *fisherman* in its reports and correspondence. According to news reports, the objectors held that the term *fisherman* "has a long and proud history dating back thousands of years." In fact, *fisherman* entered the English language only in the sixteenth century, according to the Oxford English Dictionary, whereas *fisher* was used in the ninth century to mean "a person who fishes," and it appears many times in that sense in the King James Version of the Bible. (*Fishermen* appears once.)

Fortunately the desire of some people who fish to be called "fishermen" can be respected in individual communication without subverting the purpose of sex-neutral occupational titles. The significance of the new terms is that ultimately a younger generation can grow up free from limiting concepts of "men's jobs" and "women's jobs."

It would be impossible to include in this section all the compound job titles ending in *man* for which common-gender alternatives are needed and are being sought. The examples given are intended to suggest the scope of the problem and the kinds of solutions available. Writers and speakers who are willing to experiment and perhaps come up with their own new terms or compounds will risk the wrath of the language purists, but they will be in the company of many respected writers who have added to the vitality of English.

Some Recalcitrant Compounds

When the *man* syllable comes in the middle of a word, finding a one-word alternative is hard. No one seriously suggests *sportsmanship* should be turned into *sportspersonship,* and as an alternative for *workmanlike, workerlike,* though passable, lacks force. Fortunately synonyms can usually be found:

The award is for sportsmanship.	The award is for the highest ideals of fair play.
The bricklayers did a workmanlike job.	The bricklayers did a skillful job *or* The bricklayers' work was well done.

| Their statesmanlike actions were commendable. | Their diplomatic actions (*or* tact and skill) were commendable. |

Fathers, Brothers, and BOMFOG

To describe George Washington as "the father of his country" or to speak of the authors of the United States Constitution as "the Founding Fathers" is to use sexually appropriate metaphors. But to lump all the people who came over on the *Mayflower* under the name "Pilgrim Fathers" is nonsense. Women and girls were members of the company, and the survival of the new colony depended as much on them as on their male companions. Why not simply call them all Pilgrims?

Similarly, although *Christian Fathers* is a specialized term that refers to particular men in the early church, it is inappropriate to speak of the "fathers of industry" or the "fathers of industrial medicine." The latter phrase excludes, for example, Dr. Alice Hamilton, acknowledged leader in that field, and the former ignores the inventive genius of women like Catherine Littlefield Greene, who suggested the need for a cotton gin to Eli Whitney and who may have contributed substantially to its design; Margaret E. Knight, a nineteenth-century inventor of industrial machinery; and unknown numbers of anonymous women whose creative ideas were credited to men. Common-gender nouns like *pioneers, founders, trailblazers,* and *innovators* are useful alternatives to the metaphorical "fathers" who were female as well as male.

Like *fathers,* the words *brothers, brethren,* and *brotherhood* are masculine-gender terms with standard feminine-gender equivalents. Generations of sisters have learned not to challenge the use of *brother* terms as symbols of universal human kinship. Theirs not to question why. Yet the questions remain. Does a carpenter become a "brother" when she joins a trade union calling itself a "Brotherhood"? Who is invited to take part in National Brotherhood Week? Does a billboard proclaiming that "Love Transforms Us into Brothers" mean to suggest a new approach to sex change?

"The brotherhood of man and the fatherhood of God" sounds noble—until one thinks about the people it leaves out. A few years ago reporters covering political campaigns heard the phrase so often they recorded it in their notes by initials only: BOMFOG. Shorthand for all the false generic terms and expressions that define women as nonhuman, BOMFOG, in the words of the author Eve Merriam, "continues to engulf our language and distort our thinking."

2 | The Pronoun Problem

"God send everyone their heart's desire."

Most people are taught in school that the above sentence is ungrammatical. It should be corrected, we are told, to read

God send everyone his heart's desire.

Use of the pronouns *he, his,* and *him* to refer to any unspecified or hypothetical person who may be either female or male is usually justified on two grounds. First, the practice is said to be an ancient rule of English grammar long and faithfully followed by educated speakers and writers. Second, it is asserted—somewhat paradoxically, if the usage is thought to distinguish the educated from the uneducated—that everybody knows *he* includes *she* in generalizations. Historical and psychological research in the past few years has produced evidence to refute both claims.

HISTORICAL BACKGROUND

The first grammars of modern English were written in the sixteenth and seventeenth centuries. They were mainly intended to help boys from well-to-do families prepare for the study of Latin, a language most scholars considered superior to English. The male authors of these earliest English grammars wrote for male readers in an age when

35

few women were literate. The masculine-gender pronouns they used in grammatical examples and generalizations did not reflect a belief that masculine pronouns could refer to both sexes. They reflected the reality of male cultural dominance and the male-centered world view that resulted. Males were perceived as the standard representatives of the human species, females as something else.

Although the early grammarians examined many aspects of their native tongue and framed innumerable rules governing its use, their writings contain no statement to the effect that masculine pronouns are sex-inclusive when used in general references. Not until the eighteenth century did a "rule" mandating such usage appear in an English grammar book, and not until the nineteenth century was it widely taught.

Present-day linguists, tracing the history of the so-called generic *he,* have found that it was invented and prescribed by the grammarians themselves in an attempt to change long-established English usage. The object of the grammarians' intervention was the widespread acceptance of *they* as a singular pronoun, as in Lord Chesterfield's remark (1759),

> "If a person is born of a gloomy temper . . . they cannot help it."

Nearly three centuries earlier, England's first printer, William Caxton, had written,

> "Each of them should . . . make themself ready,"

and the invocation

> "God send everyone their heart's desire"

is from Shakespeare. In such usages, grammarians argued, *they* lacked the important syntactical feature of agreement in number with a singular antecedent. But in prescribing *he* as the alternative, they dismissed as unimportant a lack of agreement in gender with a feminine antecedent.

In 1850 an Act of Parliament gave official sanction to the recently invented concept of the "generic" *he.* In the language used in acts of Parliament, the new law said, "words importing the masculine gender shall be deemed and taken to include females." Although similar language in contracts and other legal documents subsequently helped reinforce this grammatical edict in all English-speaking countries, it was often conveniently ignored. In 1879, for example, a move to admit female physicians to the all-male Massachusetts Medical Society was effectively blocked on the grounds that the society's by-laws describing membership used the pronoun *he*.

CURRENT USAGE

"The [copy] editor's duties are, in general, twofold. First, he (more often she) tries to carry out the author's wishes and edit the manuscript to his satisfaction. . . ."

—A publisher's style manual

As a linguistic device imposed on the language rather than a natural development arising from a broad consensus, "generic" *he* is fatally flawed. This fact has been demonstrated in several recent systematic investigations of how people of both sexes use and understand personal pronouns. The studies confirm that in spoken usage—from the speech of young children to the conversation of university professors—*he* is rarely intended or understood to include *she*. On the contrary, at all levels of education people whose native tongue is English seem to know that *he, him,* and *his* are gender-specific and cannot do the double duty asked of them.

This failure of masculine-gender pronouns to represent everyone becomes clear when, as in the example above, the referent of the pronoun is likely to be a woman. *She* is usually used in generalizations about secretaries, nurses, preschool teachers, baby-sitters, and shoppers, for example. Theoretically *he* should always work, but the inclination to switch to *she* in some cases demonstrates that the masculine-gender pronoun is felt to be either inadequate or ridiculous. Why? Because grammarians to the contrary, *he* brings a male image to mind, and it does so whether editors, authors, nomads, or acrobats are the subject. Like "generic" *man,* "generic" *he* fosters the misconception that the standard human being is male.

One measure of people's interest in the generic pronoun problem was the response to a nationally syndicated article on the subject by the columnist Tom Wicker, who reported that it brought "the greatest single outpouring of mail" he had ever received. Probably a better measure is the explosive increase in alternatives to "generic" *he* in all media. More and more writers and speakers seem to agree with the feeling expressed by psychologist Wendy Martyna, who wrote, " 'He' deserves to live out its days doing what it has always done best—referring to 'he' and not 'she.' "

Solving Pronoun Problems

They as a Singular

"I corrected a boy for writing 'no one . . . they' instead of 'no one . . . he,' explaining that 'no one' was singular. But he said, 'How do you know it was a he?' "

—A teacher

Children can be very logical. Although to some educated adults using *they* as a singular pronoun is like committing a crime, youngsters use it freely until someone convinces them they shouldn't. Most people, when writing and speaking informally, also rely on singular *they* as a matter of course, and so have many noted writers:

"Every person . . . now recovered their liberty."

—Oliver Goldsmith

"Nobody prevents you, do they?"

—William Makepeace Thackeray

"I shouldn't like to punish anyone, even if they'd done me wrong."   —George Eliot

". . . everyone shall delight us, and we them."

—Walt Whitman

"Now, nobody does anything well that they cannot help
doing." —John Ruskin

"It's enough to drive anyone out of their senses."
—George Bernard Shaw

"[H]e did not believe it rested anybody to lie with their
head high . . ." —Elizabeth Bowen

"You do not have to understand someone in order to love
them." —Lawrence Durrell

"And how easy the way a man or woman would come in
here, glance around, find smiles and pleasant looks waiting
for them, then wave and sit down by themselves."
—Doris Lessing

Everyday examples abound:

"Everyone raised their voice in song."

"If you have a friend or relative who would like to join,
have them fill out the coupon below and make their check
payable to . . ."

"Anyone using the beach after 5 P.M. does so at their own
risk."

Once upon a time *you* was a plural pronoun only. It
assumed its singular function (replacing *thou*) in the days
before prescriptive grammarians were around to inhibit
that kind of change. English needs a comparable third-
person singular pronoun, and for many *they* meets the
need.

Those who cannot bring themselves to use *they* in place
of *he* sometimes produce sentences like:

"Nevertheless, everyone, the fastidious queen included, resigned himself sooner or later."

In another example, an article reporting that "Eudora
Welty and Robert Penn Warren were featured luminaries
of a Forum on Southern Writing" went on to say that

"Each author also presented an evening of readings from
his own works."

In the first case, where the import of *everyone* is clearly plural, the phrase "resigned themselves" would be less jarring. In the second, "their own works" would convey equal billing more smoothly and at the same time avoid the gaffe of misrepresenting Welty's sex.

In still another instance a well-known author wrote:

> "[A] man or woman must learn to feel an emotional response before he is ready to undertake the dreadfully difficult problem of giving his love, his heart, to a being of the human kind."

Although the sexually inclusive image would have been sustained if the sentence had read

> [A] man or woman must learn to feel an emotional response before they are ready to undertake the dreadfully difficult problem of giving their love. . . .

perhaps the smell of chalk dust was so inhibiting in this case that recasting the sentence from scratch was the writer's only alternative.

He or She

Despite the charge of clumsiness, double-pronoun constructions have made a comeback, apparently on the reasonable grounds that words should reflect reality, as in the following:

> "If, however, that same trucker picks up a cargo at the Heinz plant to avoid returning home empty, he or she might well be in a pickle."   —*New York Times* editorial

> "But the average American—exercising caution, weighing the risks, never investing more than he or she can afford to lose—can at least hope to keep even, and perhaps a step or two ahead of inflation."

> —James Daniel, *Reader's Digest*

> "To be black in this country is simply too pervasive an experience for any writer to omit from her or his work. It *has* to be there in one form or another."

> —Samuel R. Delany, *The Crisis*

(In connection with Delany's unaccustomed order, see **Order,** page 93; for abbreviated forms of *he or she,* see **Further Alternatives,** page 43.)

Pluralizing

The trouble with the *he or she* form is that it becomes awkward when repeated. In order to avoid using the double-pronoun construction many times in an extended context, the writing can often be recast in the plural. The annually published catalog of a medical school, for example, formerly described the course of study undertaken by "the medical student" (who was always referred to as "he") in this way:

> "During his fourth-year studies . . . he assumes responsibilities in keeping with his stage of learning."

Nursing school catalogs of the same period invariably phrased curriculum descriptions in terms like

> As she gains experience and knowledge, the student nurse has increasing opportunities for clinical work.

When the materials are rewritten in the plural, the exclusive pronouns vanish, with the added advantage that the change both recognizes and encourages the growing numbers of women in medicine and men in nursing:

> "During their fourth-year studies . . . they assume responsibilities in keeping with their stage of learning."

> As they gain experience and knowledge, student nurses have increasing opportunities for clinical work.

She, Her, Etc., as False Generics

Feminine-gender pronouns, as used in the "student nurse" example and in *The New Yorker*'s response to the following goof, are false generics (see page 9).

> Meals are prepared under supervision of a dietician packaged in disposable sytrofoam containers.
> —*Oswego (N.Y.) Palladium-Times*

"Never mind her predicament. Are the meals any good?"

—*The New Yorker*

Eliminating Pronouns

When it is important to focus on a nonspecific individual who might be of either sex, the solution is often to drop pronouns entirely. Instead of

"A handicapped child may be able to feed and dress himself"

the sentence could be written

A handicapped child may be able to eat and get dressed without help.

A social service agency's annual report used masculine-gender terms in explaining a legal decision that affected its work with clients. In the agency's words, the court ruled that

"Information provided by a client to a social service agency is privileged in the same way as are communications between a lawyer and his client, a physician and his patient, or a clergyman and a penitent."

The sentence could have referred to

communications between lawyer and client, physician and patient, or a member of the clergy and a penitent.

In other descriptions of one-to-one relationships, replacing pronouns with nouns and articles allows for the inclusion of both sexes. In the following example, the writer made it clear that a child's psychological parent may be either male or female but failed to make equally clear that the child may also be of either sex:

"[A] child's relationship with a psychological parent, whether or not he or she is the child's natural parent, should never be interrupted. What counts in such a relationship is the child's degree of attachment and whether he feels wanted and needed—needed for himself, not for some financial advantage . . ."

A possible revision:

> [A] child's relationship with a psychological parent, whether or not he or she is the child's natural parent, should never be interrupted. What counts in such a relationship is the child's degree of attachment and feeling of being wanted and needed—needed as a person, not for some financial advantage . . .

Pronouns may also be eliminated by the device of repeating the noun.

> "Style means that the author has fused his material and his technique with the distinctive quality of his personality"

might be reworded as

> Style means that the author has fused material and technique with the distinctive quality of the author's own personality.

Sometimes the puzzle is not how to replace a pronoun, but how and why it ever crept into the sentence to start with:

> "One hundred and twenty . . . college women were asked to evaluate eight paintings on the basis of the artist's technical competence, his creativity, overall quality and content of the painting, emotion expressed, and estimation of the artist's future success."

In such a case the rhythm as well as the sense are improved when *his* is simply deleted.

Further Alternatives

Writing designed to give instructions or practical advice can avoid the third-person pronoun problem by addressing the reader directly. The financial columnist Sylvia Porter often uses this form. For example:

> "The warehouse store is another way for you to curb your soaring food bills. . . . You, the customer, do your own bagging and loading of groceries into your car."

Porter also uses abbreviated double-pronoun constructions, as in

> "After a victim of a consumer fraud discovers he/she has been ripped off . . ."

Legal contracts and other forms may be printed with *he/she, his/her,* etc., so the inapplicable pronouns can be crossed out. Some writers even favor a further abbreviation of the double-pronoun construction:

> "Any amateur psychiatrist would be more sophisticated in the use s/he made of such 'data.'"

One sometimes serves as a third-person pronoun:

> A visitor to the island can spend as little as ten dollars a day provided he is willing to give up eating.

can be recast to read

> When visiting the island, one can spend as little as ten dollars a day provided one is willing to give up eating.

The Male Animal

> "Shrike: He often hunts when he isn't hungry—but he doesn't waste the extra food. . . .

> "Dolphin: Probably the most intelligent mammal after man, this friendly and talkative creature has a built-in sonar system of his own."

These descriptions are from a mailing piece advertising an educational game for children, but the compulsion to refer to animals in masculine-gender terms is not limited to advertising copywriters. Even teachers and scientists fall into the habit of using masculine pronouns for all creatures not specifically identified as female. When an adult sees a hawk riding a thermal updraft and says to a child, "Look at him soar!" the child not only learns something about how hawks fly but also that all hawks are male and, by implication, that maleness is the norm.

In a review of a book about dinosaurs written for young children, the critic lamented the dearth of factual information provided and then said:

> "We learn just two things about Stegosaurus, for instance, that he had sharp, bony plates sticking up along his back and tail and that he ate plants."

It seems reasonable to expect, as well, that the fact-conscious reviewer not obscure the fact of Stegosaurus's sexual differentiation.

Using *it* is not offensive to animals and provides a simple way to avoid giving misinformation when generalizing or when the sex of an individual is unknown. The actual game cards referred to in the advertising copy at the beginning of this section used *it* consistently and naturally:

> "Each night the gorilla puts together a kind of bed, made of leaves, on which it sleeps through the night. It lives mainly on the ground. . . .

> "The black rhinoceros is the only member of the genus *Diceros*. Like its cousin the white rhinoceros it bears two horns. . . ."

Oddly enough, some writers continue to use *it* even when the sex of an animal is germane. An article about gamecocks, for example, used *it* throughout, although cocks are by definition male. In another instance a three-paragraph science brief began

> "When a foraging bee finds a particularly juicy clump of flowers, how does it relate that information to other bees in the hive?"

The next paragraph then explained the

> " 'waggle dance,' a series of movements in which the female bee swings her abdomen and uses her wing musculature to produce a sound."

Such a switch in midstream is not as misleading as the practice of using *he* "generically," but it is confusing. One gathers, correctly, that foraging bees who do the "waggle dance" are always female, but the *it* in paragraph one leaves open the possibility that some nondancing foragers are male.

Reporters could not seem to make up their minds what to call the great white shark that got away after being harpooned off Montauk Point, New York, in June 1978. Various skippers, marina operators, and helicopter pilots who saw the animal were quoted as calling it "he," "she," and "it." Although the reporters themselves generally favored "it," they sometimes switched to "he" in the same news item. Since the shark escaped, its sex remains unknown.

A New Generic Pronoun?

In the nineteenth century Charles Converse of Erie, Pennsylvania, proposed a new word to serve as a common-gender pronoun meaning "he or she." Converse's invention was *thon* (a contraction of *that one*) with *thon's* as the possessive, and it was carried in American dictionaries into the 1950s. It may not have been the first neologism proposed to solve the pronoun problem, and it was far from the last.

In recent years a growing conviction that English needs a new sex-inclusive singular pronoun has produced myriad suggestions, among them *co, E, tey,* and *hesh.* Some of the proposals have been used in published materials or have become part of the everyday speech of people living in egalitarian communities. In her novel *The Cook and the Carpenter* (1973), June Arnold adopted *na* as a sex-neutral pronoun, and Marge Piercy used *person,* and the shorter form *per,* in *Woman on the Edge of Time* (1976). The 1979 edition of the supervisors' guide *Managers Must Lead!* by Ray A. Killian, published by AMACOM, a division of American Management Associations, uses *hir* as a common-gender pronoun throughout. In a cogent introductory statement, the publishers explain the purpose of the innovation and the reasons for their selection of *hir.*

By the end of the 1970s, a few people were beginning to talk about an organized effort to introduce a new generic singular pronoun into English as it is spoken in the United States. The impetus for this move did not come from linguists or communications specialists. It came from psychologists whose studies had confirmed that for most native speakers of English *he*, in a generic context, does not mean "he or she." As part of this effort experimenters have been running tests with college students to assess the effectiveness of various coined words, including some of those mentioned above, as sex-inclusive pronouns. The one that proves most accessible to large numbers of test subjects—that is, the term most understandable and easy to use in a variety of sex-inclusive contexts—will be proposed for general adoption.

Proponents of this plan hope to involve influential communications media—major newspapers, magazines, and broadcasting networks—in their effort to enrich English with a new, truly generic pronoun.

3 | Generalizations

Assigning Gender to Generic Terms

> The typical American adult of the 1980s is more self-directed, more able to make thoughtful choices and grasp unexpected opportunities, than was her mother in the 1950s.

Something wrong? Not if you sanction the generic use of gender-specific terms. By a narrow statistical margin "the typical American adult" is more likely to be female than male. Nevertheless, most people would be surprised and even confused by a generalization about "American adults" phrased in terms of women.

Why, then, is it common to find similar generalizations in which masculine gender is consciously or unconsciously assigned to generic words? This one, for example, where *adult* is equated with "adult male":

> "Another difference between the Mariners and many other [fife and drum] corps is that it is strictly an adult group. It does not take in either women or students who are still in high school."

What the author presumably meant was

> Another difference between the Mariners and many other corps is that it is limited to men (*or* to adult males).

48

In another case a Southern author, writing satirically about how the rest of the country views Southerners, asked,

> "Who are these people? What are they like? Do they have any pastimes besides fighting, hunting, drinking and writing novels? Do they really sleep with their sisters and bay at the moon?"

At least some Southern women fight, hunt, drink, and write novels, but since the writer was apparently thinking only of Southern men, it would have been more accurate either to say so or, as an alternative, to even the score by providing a brace of equally ironic questions about women:

> Who are these people? What are they like? Do they have any pastimes besides fighting, hunting, drinking and writing novels? Do their men really sleep with their sisters and bay at the moon? Do their women wear crinolines and stash their whiskey behind the camellias?

Men, in particular, seem to forget that "the average person" and "the species" are not limited to one sex. A newspaper columnist writes of the almost limitless number of human activities an "average person" crams into the space of one year:

> "The average person finds it no problem at all to have three head colds, one sunburn, an attack of athlete's foot, 20 headaches, three hangovers and five temper tantrums with adolescent children, and still get in his 61 hours of shaving. . . ."

Another, who would like to do away with neckties, writes:

> "But what earthly purpose is served by tying a knot around your neck every day just so you can look like every other member of the species?"

And a book reviewer describes H. G. Wells's ability to

> "exert his magnetism on the small boy in all of us."

In such cases, solutions are not difficult:

> "the average person"

could be ·

> the average male;
>
> "every other member of the species"

could be

> every other man;

and

> "the small boy in all of us"

could be

> the child in all of us.

Or, if the writer really means "the average person," an alternative to the clause on shaving might be something like "and still get in their 61 hours in the shower." What is less easy is to convince writers prone to androcentrism of the need to guard against it.

In a factual account, unconscious exclusion of one sex or the other can actually distort the information being presented. Sometimes the results, though frustrating, are amusing. A syndicated newspaper story on the Abkhasian people of Soviet Georgia, many of whom live vigorous lives well past their hundredth birthdays, included this description:

> "They appear strikingly fit, unusually erect from long years on horseback, short but lean. Most have their own teeth under flamboyant silver mustaches."

Since nowhere in the thousand-word story did the writer refer specifically to women, the puzzled reader is left to wonder whether the fabled Abkhasian longevity is characteristic of male Abkhasians only. Or is one supposed to believe that both sexes sport flamboyant silver mustaches?

Similar absurdities arise when writers unconsciously assign gender to other proper nouns like *Americans* or *the French.*

> Sharing our railway compartment were two Norwegians and their wives

might be stated, just as accurately,

> Sharing our railway compartment were two Norwegians and their husbands

or, more concisely,

> Sharing our railway compartment were two Norwegian couples.

More often, the assignment of gender to common-gender nouns has serious consequences, as when terms like *colonists, immigrants, slaves, settlers, pioneers,* and *farmers* are used in contexts that refer to males only:

> In the nineteenth century immigrants were met at the dock by party politicians who promised them jobs in exchange for their votes when they became citizens.

What the sentence really means, as we know from history, is

> In the nineteenth century immigrants were met at the dock by party politicians who promised jobs in exchange for the votes of the men when they became citizens.

Similarly,

> The Fifteenth Amendment was intended to insure the voting rights of former slaves

means

> The Fifteenth Amendment was intended to insure the voting rights of men who had been slaves.

The long-range effects of that kind of semantic carelessness are hard to assess, but immediate effects can be concrete and readily observed. A case in point involves the word *farmer.* According to John J. Gilligan, former administrator of the United States Agency for International Development, from 40 to 70 percent of farmers in Third World countries are women. Until recently, however, these women were frequently excluded from projects designed to assist farmers in developing countries because, as Gilligan discovered, "Western development experts simply assumed that farmers were male."

Closer to home, the Internal Revenue Service has been known to make the same assumption. In 1978, newspapers reported a federal district court decision in favor of a woman who built up a sizable farm operation with her husband during their forty-three years of marriage. When her husband died, the IRS held that all the farm equipment had belonged to him and thus was included in his estate. But the court ruled that the woman was equally responsible for the farm's success: she kept the books, marketed eggs, hauled cattle, cared for the hired hands, and helped harvest the grain. Declaring that it would not ignore

> "this farm wife's contribution to the success of the business,"

the court ordered the IRS to give her back some $40,000 of estate tax, plus interest. It seems clear, however, that if the IRS and the court had thought not in terms of "this farm wife's" contribution but rather of

> this farmer's contribution to the success of the business,

she would have been considered a full partner from the beginning, and the case might never have arisen.

The inability of many people to see women as farmers and farmers as women has led to belittling terms like *farmerette* and *farmeress*. (See **"Feminine" Suffixes,** page 109.) If a writer has reason to identify farmers by sex, *farm women* and *farm men* are useful parallel terms subsumed under the common-gender noun *farmer*.

Linguistic Abuse of *Wives*

> "The forces that keep the corporate wife in her place are powerful. . . ."

> "Once Senate wives rolled bandages for World War I wounded. Now they meet regularly to make nonpolitical

talk along with hand puppets and clothing for a Washington children's hospital."

Terms like *corporate wives* and *Senate wives* reflect the continuing reality of male power preserves. Women thus identified as appendages both of a man and of an institution are usually expected to accept a well-defined role on behalf of the institution, and, in the case of the *corporate wife,* to function in ways that in effect provide the corporation with two employees for the price of one. But since increasing numbers of women whose husbands hold high-level posts are pursuing careers of their own, terms like *Senate wives* and *corporate wives* have meaning only when they are used in such contexts as those quoted above.

> Senate wife Mary Able is a professor of biochemistry at XYZ University

is a misuse of *Senate wife,* for the point is not that Mary Able is married to a senator but that she teaches biochemistry. If Senator Able is to be mentioned at all, an alternative might be

> Mary Able, whose husband is Senator Harry Able, is . . .

or

> Mary Able is a professor of biochemistry at XYZ University. She and her husband, Senator Harry Able, . . .

Faculty wives, a familiar term a generation ago, has pretty much given way to *faculty spouses* at schools where women teach in more than token numbers. Similarly, *service wives* sounds increasingly dated as more women enter the military and other government services. In reporting the moment when Jimmy Carter embraced Leonid Brezhnev after signing the second strategic arms limitation treaty, *New York Times* correspondent Craig R. Whitney wrote:

> "The gesture evoked cheers and applause from the hundreds of diplomats, delegation members, their spouses and journalists who gathered for the historic signing."

Corporate wives and even *Senate wives* may also be traveling the road to obsolescence. (See **Women as Entities, Not Appendages,** page 90.)

Fortunately the mention of wives sometimes performs an unexpected but valuable linguistic service: it blows the whistle on a writer who is unconsciously assigning masculine gender to a generic word. Here are a few examples:

"The American adult goes into a world that does not 'owe him a living' . . . and the only person he will be able to trust when he gets out there will be his little wife. . . ."

"I suppose any normal American would rather sit with his wife in a public place than apart from her. . . ."

"There's no real commonality among programmers. I don't know that we beat our wives any more than anyone else."

"It's the great secret of doctors, known only to their wives . . . that most things get better by themselves. . . ."

And a book about "America's sexual revolution" is titled

Thy Neighbor's Wife.

Gratuitous Modifiers

As Putdowns

"Powerful lady attorney and confident young lawyer team up to defend a wealthy contractor accused of murder."
—TV listing

Question: What sex are the confident young lawyer and the wealthy contractor?

If for some reason identifying the sex of the protagonists in a television show about lawyers is important, why did the listing not read

Powerful attorney and her young male colleague team up to defend a wealthy businessman accused of murder.

The answer is that in our culture we are not inclined to diminish a man's prestige. Nor should we be. But that is what labeling someone with an incidental characteristic like sex or color or national origin does. In real life competence depends on things like training, experience, talent, and personality, and these are qualities the words *powerful* and *confident* suggest. Using a gratuitous modifier like *lady* to shift attention from what is genuinely relevant to what will titillate television viewers may be an accepted ploy in the ratings game. But even so, should it always be done at the expense of women?

Sometimes, as in the television example, gratuitous modifiers are used purposely. More often they slip in as a result of unconscious prejudice or out of habit, and yet the results are equally negative.

> "But I got a contrary reaction from a woman attorney I talked to who is an expert in the field. . . . 'You are doing a foolhardy thing,' she said."

could have been

> But I got a contrary reaction from another attorney I talked to who is an expert in the field. . . .

Since the reader will discover from the feminine-gender pronoun the incidental fact that the expert referred to is a woman, the qualifier was as superfluous as the interpolated words *a man* would have been in another sentence from the same account:

> "I rushed to the pay phone in the hall and started phoning lawyers I knew until I found one, *a man,* who was in his office."

In activities or professional fields where men are outnumbered by women, they are the ones who get the gratuitous modifiers, and with the same result:

> Walt Whitman was a male nurse during the Civil War

could have been

> Walt Whitman was a nurse during the Civil War.

As with women, such a sex qualifier is usually unnecessary. Its suggestion that "male nurses," "male secretaries," or "male kindergarten teachers" are not *real* nurses, secretaries, or kindergarten teachers is demeaning, and the implication that people who hold those jobs are always female is no more true today than the equally false assumption that all lawyers, doctors, and engineers are male. The following example illustrates the basic message conveyed, namely that what is identified by a superfluous sex qualifier is a deviation from the standard:

> "This formidable five-eyed female may eat her mate for dinner. . . . She's the female praying mantis."

Is a female praying mantis not a true member of her species? If one grants that she is, why not let the pronouns indicate her sex?

> This formidable five-eyed creature may eat her mate for dinner. . . . She's the praying mantis.

Were the dining proclivities of female and male praying mantises reversed, would anyone be likely to add the redundant adjective *male?*

> This formidable five-eyed male may eat his mate for dinner. . . . He's the male praying mantis.

Those tempted to say yes may be surprised that lexicographers do not necessarily agree. After describing bowerbirds in terms of taxonomy and location, for example, Webster's Second Unabridged Dictionary continues,

> "They build *bowers* or *runs* . . . which are used as playhouses and to attract the females. . . .

The wording in Webster's Third (1966) also implies by omission that the male bowerbird is the standard:

> "any of a group of . . . passerine birds . . . of the Australian region that build chambers or passages . . . used as playhouses or to attract the females. . . ."

Not until the 1974 Collegiate do the Merriam-Webster editors admit females to full bowerbirddom:

> "any of various passerine birds . . . of the Australian region in which the male builds a chamber or passage . . . used esp. to attract the female."

This example is not an isolated one. A popular bird identification book provides photographs of "the cardinal" and "the ♀ cardinal," and several dictionaries define certain species of deer (e.g., the fallow deer) with reference to their antlers without making clear that antlers are characteristic of the male only.

Usage arbiters at the *New York Times* took a look in 1979 at what is implied when *woman* is used gratuitously as a modifier. After three items had appeared in the same column of news briefs mentioning, respectively, "women students," a "woman photographer," and a "woman customer," an in-house bulletin from the news desk commented: "The use of *woman* as a modifier suggests that such words as *student, photographer* and *customer,* unadorned, are masculine. . . . [P]robably the time has come to banish *woman* as an adjective; we don't use *man* that way. When a person's sex is truly newsworthy, let us use the same kinds of construction for both sexes: *male students, female students; lawyers who are women, lawyers who are men."*

Unintentional Distortion

Gratuitous modifiers can also distort meaning. The author of an article on Dunbar High School, the first public high school for blacks in the United States, described one graduate of the days when Dunbar was still segregated as

"the first black general in the United States Army"
and another as
"one of the nation's leading black historians."

In the first instance the adjective *black* was appropriate; in the second it was not. The author may have meant

one of the nation's leading authorities on black history
or
a black who is one of the nation's leading historians
or
a leader among the nation's historians who are black.

When, as above, the use of a modifier obscures the question of whether the person referred to is being judged on a par with everyone else or only within a limited category, it is particularly damaging. In an article on Alicia de Larrocha, the critic Donal Henahan said that to call her "the greatest woman pianist of our day . . . serves, like most labels, to discourage thought." It skirts the question, Henahan wrote, of whether de Larrocha "might actually be one of the finest living pianists. . . . [It] diminishes de Larrocha's achievements by ghettoizing them."

"Damn Good for a Woman"

The youngster who says, "I ate all my broccoli and didn't even say how much I hate it" is skilled at apophasis, which Webster's Second Unabridged defines as "mention of something in disclaiming intention to mention it." Apophasis can also be an effective, if somewhat underhanded, political device, as when a candidate says, "I do not intend to make an issue of my opponent's lavish personal expense account." But when speakers or writers try to use it to beat the gratuitous modifier, apophasis backfires:

> "She is the kind of judge who no one would say is a 'woman judge'—she's a judge."

> "No one will ever call her a 'lady anthropologist.' "

Such expressions suggest that women who excel professionally are double aberrations: as women ("She can't be a real professional") and as professionals ("She can't be a real woman").

> She is an excellent judge

and

> She is a first-rate anthropologist

are direct and free of the implication "Damn good for a woman." The writer A. Alvarez managed to get his message across without casting any aspersions when he wrote of the late Jean Rhys,

> "To my mind, she is, quite simply, the best living English novelist."

Relevance and Irrelevance

In some circumstances sex, like race, may be a significant part of the information to be conveyed:

> "Margaret Thatcher won a governing majority today as Europe's first woman prime minister."

> On October 2, 1967, Thurgood Marshall became the first black justice of the Supreme Court of the United States.

But this information need not be repeated endlessly. Once barriers have been breached and stereotypes dispelled, race and sex become secondary. Then the person who achieves distinction deserves to be identified primarily on the basis of merit. Instead of

> Dr. John Adams, a prominent black pediatrician, has been named medical director of Children's Hospital. Other staff changes this month include the retirement of Dr. Paul Zenkel as chief of the Cardiac Service. He will be replaced by a woman, Dr. Harriet Mooney

a nonracist, nonsexist version would read:

> Dr. John Adams, a prominent pediatrician, has been named medical director of Children's Hospital. In other staff changes this month, Dr. Paul Zenkel retires as chief of the Cardiac Service, and Dr. Harriet Mooney becomes the new chief.

Sports Reporting

The headline on a newspaper story about two track and field events, the Memorial Relays held in Teaneck, New Jersey, and the Nanuet Relays held in Nanuet, New York, reads:

> "Schoolboys Struggle Against Chill, Rain"

For six paragraphs the wording seems appropriate. Then comes a paragraph beginning:

> "In the girls' competition at the Memorial Relays . . ."

The rest of the story deals only with boys' events; if girls competed at Nanuet, they were not mentioned.

This ho-hum approach to schoolgirl sports is common. The attitude of some reporters seems to be that girls (and women) don't count since they are rarely competitive with boys (and men), who do count. But that is like saying heavyweight bouts are the only real boxing contests when in fact the International Olympic Committee awards gold, silver, and bronze medals to men in eleven different classes, and at last count the World Boxing Association and the World Boxing Council both recognized twelve championship divisions for men from Junior Flyweight on up. It is this recognition of individual and class differences that sportswomen also merit.

Fortunately the last few years have brought a marked change in the amount of space allotted to women's contests, and—equally important—the language sportswriters use in describing women's events is becoming more evenhanded. Writers cannot completely counteract the putdown implicit in such nonparallel titles as the Professional Golfers Association and the Ladies Professional Golfers Association, or the National Collegiate Athletic Association and the Alliance of Intercollegiate Athletics for Women. However today's trend toward separate divisions for women and men under one overall organization helps: men's swimming and women's swimming, men's gymnastics and women's gymnastics, women's and men's archery, handball, alpine skiing, figure skating, and so forth. That is the Olympic tradition, and it has also been adopted by a growing number of schools and colleges. A college magazine, for example, reports:

> "The men's hockey program . . . has experienced a notable revival of spirit and support in the past two seasons. . . ."

> "The women's swim team opened its season with a road victory over . . ."

This kind of parallel treatment does not deny that in intercollegiate sports some men's competitions result in a bigger gate than all women's contests put together, but it acknowledges that unless the sole purpose of college athletics is to make money, women deserve more than token recognition.

The same is true at the high school level where the kind of writing represented by the first example that follows is gradually giving way to the second, and in the process building interest in long-neglected girls' contests.

> Oakville High's basketball team will play Smithtown this Thursday, and the girls' basketball team will meet Smithtown's girls on Friday. Varsity coach Al Heinz said, "We have what it takes, and we're about to prove it. . . ." Since Thursday's game is the last one before the divisional playoffs, Oakville fans hope Heinz knows what he's talking about.

> Oakville High's varsity basketball teams will meet Smithtown this week, the boys Thursday and the girls Friday. Al Heinz, the boys' coach, said, "We have what it takes, and we're about to prove it. . . ." Oakville girls' coach Sally Gordon wasn't pulling a long face either. . . .

In reporting women's and girls' athletics it is no more necessary to mention the players' sex in the headline and in every other paragraph than it is to refer to the sex of male players. Since feminine-gender pronouns and the players' names speak for themselves, repeated reference to "the girls," "Oakville's girl players," or "these talented young women" slows the pace and distracts the reader. So does the use of social titles:

> "Finding pinpoint accuracy with her swift rival at net, Mrs. Lloyd continued to send shots whizzing past Miss Navratilova, finally evening the score at 5–5. Miss Navratilova hit two sizzling overheads and an ace to save her next serve and she then took the set. . . ."

If the game had been between men, the players, after their initial identification, would have been called by their last names:

> "The third set was evenly played through the first four games, but Connors seemed to take control after two lob

> smashes broke Vilas at deuce in the fifth game. Connors then held his serve for a 4–2 lead."

First-rate sports reporting, whether of a major-league baseball game or a high school soccer match, concentrates on the game and the players, not on their sex or marital situation. (See also **Names and Titles,** page 95, and **The Social Titles** *Mrs., Miss,* **and** *Ms.,* page 100.)

In sports writing, as in other fields, gratuitous modifiers can also distort meaning.

> Nancy Lopez is an outstanding woman golfer who held the 1978 rookie winnings record

implies that Lopez held the record for women. She did, but she also held the winnings record of the year for all rookie golfers regardless of sex.

> Nancy Lopez is an outstanding golfer who made more money in 1978 than any other rookie golfer of either sex

makes her achievement clear.

Personification

Signs of the times:

> In a *Ladies Home Journal* cartoon by Henry Martin, a woman in a convertible pulls up to a gas pump and says to the attendant "Fill him up!"

> The National Weather Service alters its twenty-five-year practice of identifying all hurricanes by women's first names. Every other one now blows in as the namesake of a man. It's Anna, Bob, Claudette, David, etc.

> A U.S. Navy study group on sex and minority discrimination is reported to be considering—among other things—whether the Navy should stop calling its ships "she." In a Bill Kitchen cartoon accompanying that news item, a pair of male sailors in a bar clutch their beer steins as one queries the other anxiously: "Where's it all going to end, Simpson? Where's it all going to end?"

The question some people might be tempted to ask first is, where did it all begin? Neither Simpson nor anyone else knows the answer, of course, for personification began long before recorded history. Among the earliest artifacts known to archaeologists are human representations, assumed to be of deities, indicating that for millennia God was personified as female. Today most religions, while insisting that God has no sex, rely heavily on male symbols for the Godhead (including the linguistic symbols *Father* and *He*), reserving female ones for subordinate entities like the Church.

This patriarchal religious tradition strongly influenced the development of the English language and the outlook of its speakers. In 1646 J. Poole, a grammarian, explained that "The Masculine is more worthy than the Feminine, and the Feminine is more worthy than the Neuter," and in 1795 another grammarian, L. Murray, had this to say of personification:

> Figuratively, in the English tongue, we commonly give the masculine gender to nouns which are conspicuous for the attributes of imparting or communicating, and which are by nature strong and efficacious. Those, again, are made feminine which are conspicuous for the attributes of containing or bringing forth, or which are peculiarly beautiful or amiable. Upon these principles the sun is always masculine, and the moon, because the receptacle of the sun's light, is feminine. The earth is generally feminine. A ship, a country, a city, &c. are likewise made feminine, being receivers or containers. Time is always masculine, on account of its mighty efficacy. Virtue is feminine from its beauty, and its being the object of love. Fortune and the church are generally put in the feminine gender. . . .

Today personification is applied to fewer things and, as Simpson's friend was aware, its supposed verities are less eternal. A newspaper account of the Coast Guard icebreaker-tug *Katmai Bay*, which operates on Lake Superior, consistently referred to the ship as "she." The ship's skipper, however, was quoted as follows:

"Working side by side, two of these ships could handle any ice the Great Lakes can dish up. If one gets stuck, it backs up while the other charges ahead. Then it in turn charges."

In a television science program on the wreck of the *Amoco Cadiz,* a disaster that resulted in a massive oil spill along the coast of Brittany in 1978, the narrator sometimes referred to the doomed tanker as "it," sometimes as "she." In describing the wreck itself, however, he used imagery that was both anthropomorphic and female:

"Less than a mile offshore, the Amoco Cadiz was steadily hemorrhaging into the sea. . . . Fourteen hours later, the ship impaled herself on the rocks."

Disasters are frequently personified as female. Public pressure was responsible for the National Weather Service decision to divvy up "responsibility" for the devastation caused by hurricanes, and the significance of the switch became clear as soon as hurricanes Bob, David, Fred, and Henri hit the headlines in 1979. Not only did newscasters and weather reporters show reluctance to personify them in negative imagery, but as the *NOW National Times* commented: "After the early 'him-icane' jokes . . . wore off, most radio and television weather forecasters made 'Bob' a genderless 'it' in record time. It was nothing like the old days when hurricanes with female names were known to 'flirt with the Florida coast,' were 'perfectly formed,' had tempers that 'teased and threatened.' "

But "Mother Nature" still gets "her" lumps. An ad for a rustproofing-compound for automobiles shows the picture of a vicious-looking woman with long, blood-red fingernails, and the copy reads:

"Don't let Mother Nature rip you off! She's out to kill your car's new finish. . . . Stop her. . . ."

Nuclear power plants are also female by implication. The March 1979 accident at the Three Mile Island plant in

Pennsylvania led to discussion of conditions at that facility's "sister" (never "brother") plants across the country. Similarly the product of an element's radioactive decay is known as the element's "daughter."

In English the personification of objects and ideas has more rhetorical impact than in languages where every noun has grammatical gender. A German translation of the woman saying to the gas station attendant "Fill him up!" wouldn't even get a chuckle in Bonn because *Kraftwagen,* the German word for *automobile,* is a masculine-gender noun and takes a masculine pronoun as a matter of course. The French word *navire,* meaning "ship," is also masculine, so a ship is referred to as "he" *(il)* in France, as is a parsnip, a refrigerator, and a flowerpot—all without sexual connotation.

The other notable aspect of personification in English is that many more things are represented as female than male. Just as men have influenced our language more than women have, so their fantasies have more often assigned characteristics of the "other" sex to nonliving things. When personified at all, virtuous concepts like justice and liberty are still (gallantly) accorded femaleness, whereas all-powerful forces like time and death are still male. Centers of action, the sun and the mind, are still stereotypically male; their more passive counterparts, the moon and the soul, still female. Except in art and poetry, however, entities like justice, time, the soul, and the sun are rarely represented as though they have sexual attributes. In everyday English the largest category where personification persists is that of vehicles and mechanized contraptions, all of which are sometimes called "she."

It is easy to argue that

> She's the most beautiful boat in the harbor

or

> She sails like a bird

imply compliments to women, but the sexual association is less flattering when someone refers to a cranky piece of equipment as a "bitch" or advises a friend trying to start an old motor to

> Give her a kick and she'll turn over.

"Herman," the mechanized device used at nuclear installations to perform tasks that would expose human beings to intolerable levels of radiation, is an exception to the "machines are female" assumption. Perhaps the tradition that the mind is male still predominates—even when the "mind" is a robot's.

Personifications, like other arbitrary classifications, grow out of cultural preconceptions. A few are innocuous, some destructive, but all, in common with other forms of stereotyping, can work to discourage fresh perceptions. Writers who use *it* to identify something inanimate are not tempted to rely on supposedly universal sex-linked characteristics to make their point. Instead, they must find precise words to delineate the thing itself.

4 | Seeing Women and Girls as People

Masculinity, *Femininity*, **and Other Sex-Linked Descriptives**

The characteristics we habitually identify as "womanly" and "feminine"—receptivity, tenderness, and nurturance, to name a few of the positive ones—can also characterize men. And contrary to conventional wisdom, women share such "manly" and "masculine" attributes as boldness, vigor, directness, and courage. These adjectives and their associates, terms like *masculinity* and *femininity, manliness* and *womanliness,* have become so overlaid with societal dogmas setting forth what women and men "should" be like as to have lost almost all meaning. Whose "should" are we talking about, and how do we know from one use to the next what subjective cast these sex-linked words are intended to convey?

What was meant, for example, when one important federal official said of another,

> "She seems to be able to blend a high professional standing and ability with an undeniable femininity. And she is also as tough as nails."

Was the speaker using *femininity* to mean "tenderness" or "nurturance"? Judging by the second sentence, it would appear he was not. Since "seems to be able to blend" implies a potential discrepancy between "femininity" and "high professional standing and ability," perhaps his intended meaning was something like

> She seems to be able to blend a high professional standing and ability with modest self-effacement . . . (*or* undeniable coquettishness . . . *or* an air of helpless fragility).

But those images do not go with "tough as nails" either. If the speaker meant he found his colleague appealing sexually, he might have phrased his comment

> She seems to be able to blend a high professional standing and ability with undeniable sex appeal.

Whatever the speaker's intention, the silliness of *femininity* in this context becomes obvious when a male subject is substituted:

> He seems to be able to blend a high professional standing and ability with an undeniable masculinity.

A little comparative checking in current dictionaries shows that we tend to use words like *manly* and *masculine* to connote human qualities most people aspire to, qualities like bravery and strength of character. In the definitions of these masculine-gender words, few if any negative attributes are mentioned. In contrast, words like *womanly* and *feminine* connote qualities assigned to women as women. In addition to positive ones like tenderness and receptivity, the definers frequently imply that what typically makes someone "womanly" are many not-so-admirable characteristics, among them weakness, petulance, timidity, and fickleness. Women, it is true, are often weak, petulant, timid, and fickle. But what is concealed in our lexicon of sex-linked adjectives is that men are too. In short, women are linguistically saddled with their human failings, men are linguistically disassociated from theirs.

One result of this dichotomy is that English lacks active, strong words to use specifically of women. Does the sentence

Assemblywoman Gray's campaign was notable for her
womanly response to her critics

mean

Assemblywoman Gray's campaign was notable for her gracious response to her critics.

If so it would be well to use the specific word *gracious*,
for *womanly* might be interpreted as equivalent to any of
a number of other female-associated terms frequently used
of women in politics: *abrasive, emotional*, and *strident* among
them.

Nor would one speak of

Golda Meir's womanful determination to carry on despite
her illness

in the same way one might speak of

John Wayne's manful fight against cancer.

Yet these two human beings shared a brand of courage
and determination the word *manful* brings to mind as no
comparable feminine-gender term succeeds in doing.

Recently at least one of the feminine-gender adjectives
has been showing signs of acquiring new connotations of
inner strength and resourcefulness. The phrase

"the womanly art of directing turbines"

appeared in an advertisement featuring an electrical engi-
neer who is a woman. Although the copywriter's intent
is not crystal clear, at least the use of *womanly* in this context
adds a welcome dimension to the "qualities esp. associated
with the ideal wife or mother" which one dictionary,
published in 1963, gives as special connotations of the
term.

When a governor, seeking support for his tax proposals,
asked legislators to

"be manly enough or womanly enough to stand up and
vote for these taxes"

he also used *womanly* in a still-novel way. He might have conveyed his meaning more succinctly by asking the legislators to

> be courageous enough to stand up and vote for these taxes.

Or it may be his inclusion of women was an afterthought. If so, he managed in one breath to get his foot out of his mouth and, by attaching to *womanly* the qualities now defined under *manly*, to give women their just due.

On the whole, as these examples show, sex-linked adjectives are not very useful in describing the human traits and qualities both sexes share: they are too elusive and subjective to be precise, and they arrogate to one sex attributes both possess. Although it is sometimes hard to pick words that exactly convey the meaning intended, making the effort almost always guarantees clearer writing.

Girls, Ladies, Females, Women

It sometimes takes a well-tuned ear to make appropriate choices from among the everyday words used for female human beings. One problem is that all these words have psychic overtones: of immaturity and dependence in the case of *girl;* of decorum and conformity in the case of *lady;* of sexuality and reproduction in the case of both *female* and *woman*. But all have been invested with other meanings as well, both positive and negative, and no one knows for sure which way any one of them is moving—into the mainstream or out. The following observations, then, are primarily intended to provide perspective. In this area, perhaps more than in any other, the question to ask in making choices is whether the comparable masculine-gender term would or would not be appropriate.

Girl and Gal

What separates the women from the girls—linguistically as well as biologically—is age. A person may appropriately be called a "girl" until her middle or late teens. After that, although her family and close friends may go on calling her a girl with impunity, most red-blooded women find the term offensive. Just as *boy* can be blatantly offensive to minority men, arousing feelings of helplessness and rage, so *girl* can have comparable patronizing and demeaning implications for women.

The young police officer who calls out "Good morning, girls" to two middle-aged women may intend no insult, but his greeting is an affront just the same: one adult has treated two other adults as children, and they have no adequate riposte. Similarly business executives who make pompous statements like

I'll have my girl run off some copies right away

are enhancing their own self-image at the expense of someone else's.

I'll ask my secretary (*or* assistant *or* Ms. Blake) to run off some copies right away

conveys respect and recognition. Women in full-time office jobs may be assistants, clerks, secretaries, executives, bookkeepers, managers, etc., but unless their employers are violating the child labor laws, they are rarely girls.

How strongly women feel about being called "girls" was indicated when United Technologies, as part of a corporate-image series, took a full-page advertisement in the *Wall Street Journal* headed "Let's Get Rid of 'The Girl.'" Other ads in the same series drew numerous requests for reprints, but the ad that ended, " 'The girl' is certainly a woman when she's out of her teens. Like you, she has a name. Use it" brought the greatest response of all, including congratulatory telephone calls, telegrams, and even flowers.

College and university women are not girls either, and today the "career girl" is as rare a bird as the "career boy." A brochure advertising

Ideal Luggage for the Career Girl

would almost certainly attract fewer buyers than would the claim

> Ideal Luggage for the Business Woman

One accepted use of *boy* for an adult male occurs in the British term *old boy,* meaning a graduate of a preparatory school. This usage has been imported to the United States in *the old-boy network,* an expression that describes the exclusive, informal system long used by upper-class men to help their old school buddies into positions of power. Today the small but growing number of women in high-level corporate and government posts also constitute a network, and they are helping other women onto the job ladder and up the rungs. Thus, as in this *Washington Post* story, a new use of *girl* has become eminently appropriate:

> " 'Old-Girl Network'
> Helps Women Gain High Posts
> "In and around the time-honored 'old-boy network,' which has tended to elude or exclude them, the 'girls' are weaving their own web of firstname acquaintanceships. . . ."

A variation of *girl,* often used by writers or speakers who sense that *girl* would be resented, is *gal.* Since *gal* is *girl* in disguise, using it is apt to be an out-of-the-frying-pan-into-the-fire solution. However, *gal* may possibly be useful in the kind of context that makes *guy* acceptable (a "guys and gals" sort of ambience), and it can sometimes serve well when deliberately chosen for its incongruity. Referring to an active ninety-year-old as "a feisty old gal," for example, might be paying her a greater compliment than "feisty oldster" or "plucky senior citizen" would ever succeed in doing.

Lady

Lady is used most effectively to evoke a certain standard of propriety, correct behavior, or elegance. In Jennie Churchill's words,

> "You may be a princess or the richest woman in the world, but you cannot be more than a lady."

Because of these strong connotations, *lady* is not a synonym for *woman* in the primary sense of that word any more than *gentleman* is a synonym for *man.*

> A Phoenix lady has been named to the Liquor Commission

is arch. A better choice would be

> A Phoenix woman has been named . . .

or, using an appropriate identification,

> A former president of the American Red Cross in Phoenix has been named to the Liquor Commission.

However, *lady* can successfully suggest a certain éclat, as in

> My grandmother smokes cigars like a lady.

Used informally in descriptive phrases, the noun can also imply sophistication and gutsy determination:

> Patricia Roberts Harris is one terrific lady.

Honorary epithets like *first lady* and *leading lady* reflect esteem, but when incorporated in a job title, *lady* usually implies a lesser valuation. One never hears a congresswoman referred to as a "congresslady," and *cleaning lady* or *forelady* convey a condescension lacking in the more forthright *cleaning woman, cleaner, forewoman,* and *supervisor.* Similarly a woman in real estate who handles the sale of a $10-million office building is more likely to be called a "saleswoman," "sales agent," or "sales representative" than a "saleslady."

Like other unnecessary words, *lady* has a diminishing effect when dragged in:

> Her colleagues know her as a fighting lady to be reckoned with

is stronger as

> Her colleagues know her as a fighter to be reckoned with.

When used as an adjective, *lady* often signals "this woman is not to be taken seriously" (see **Gratuitous Modifiers,** page 54). A television newscaster who reported

> "In Moscow a lady streetcleaner has been arrested for fraud. . . ."

was ostensibly telling a straight story about someone who failed to deliver after accepting money to find people apartments. If the newscaster had begun

> In Moscow, a streetcleaner has been arrested for fraud. . . .

and let pronouns indicate the streetcleaner's sex, he would have avoided giving the impression that he was ridiculing a woman because of her job—one, as it happens, many women hold in the Soviet Union. If the caveat seems strained, imagine a similar story about a "gentleman streetcleaner."

A mail-order catalog copywriter may have discouraged sales of one item by describing it as a

> "Ladies' Tool Kit."

The kit pictured contained a hammer, pliers, utility knife, five wrenches, and a screwdriver handle with six interchangeable blades—the kind of items anyone of either sex might find handy to have around the house. A more appropriate description would have been

> Home Tool Kit.

As one catalog recipient who does her own home repairs said, "Calling it a 'ladies' tool kit' means to me the tools are probably more showy than useful." The remark might apply equally to items labeled "ladies' fly rod," "ladies' typewriter," or "ladies' razor"—all of which, rightly or wrongly, inadvertently advertise themselves as flimsy versions of standard items.

Yet in other contexts *ladies,* used as a modifier, can be effective. For example, a sign saying

> Ladies' Hairdresser

may have more cachet for some potential customers than "Women's Hairdresser," and it does no harm. A woman who has her hair dressed may well be a lady in the sense that Americans have always used the terms *ladies* and *gentlemen:* not to refer to family pedigree but to acknowledge a self-image or, sometimes, to inculcate one. As usual, one test of appropriateness is whether or not the parallel masculine-gender word sounds natural.

In the adjective *ladylike* the positive associations of *lady* are usually obscured by negative ones. A reviewer of the published memoirs of Eleanor Roosevelt commented, for example, that the book's format

> "enables the reader to follow the growth of her personality and outlook, from ladylike clichés to statesmanlike judgments."

The difficulty here is not only the use of *ladylike* to mean "ineffectual" or "meaningless"; it is also the juxtaposition of a negative, female-associated word with a positive, male-associated one. An alternative might have been

> . . . from empty clichés to considered judgments.

Female

Used either as a noun or adjective, *female* is appropriate when the corresponding choice for the other sex would be *male:*

> Maggie had her puppies last night, three females and two males

sounds natural, whereas

> The Festival String Quintet includes two females

does not. On the other hand, *female* is frequently used for human beings in technical contexts:

> Insurance company actuarial charts indicate that females live longer than males

is more precise, if the statistics cover all ages, than

> Insurance company actuarial charts indicate that women live longer than men.

And

> "The primary reproductive organs or gonads of the female consist of a pair of ovaries"

is the accepted language of biology and medicine when referring to any vertebrate species, human or otherwise.

This association with medicine, health care, and other institutional contexts like law enforcement could explain why *female* and *male* frequently sound a wrong note.

> The two female suspects were held on $50,000 bonds

may be the prescribed form for a police report, but in ordinary writing

> Both women were held on $50,000 bonds

is less clinical.

Woman

Obviously, *woman* is the most useful all-around word for referring to adult female people:

> The jury of seven women and five men was chosen quickly.
>
> Their new advertising campaign is directed at women.
>
> She's an attractive woman with a colorful, confident style.

For a person somewhere between girlhood and woman-hood—often a variable and subjective state—*woman* can always be qualified by *young*, either when it might sound strange or inappropriate to use the term by itself, as in

> She's only eleven, but she has the presence of a young woman,

or when a substitute for *girl* is desirable:

> We are trying to expand our readership to include young women in the thirteen- to sixteen-year age-group.

One of the problems with *woman* is that, like other female-associated words, it is frequently used as a modifier when no modifier is called for (see page 54ff.). Unlike

> Many women choose to go to a woman doctor, just as many men prefer a man doctor,

which makes a valid distinction, *woman* is forever ending up in some mindless cliché like *woman driver,* that implied canard refuted long ago by statistics.

Used as a noun, *woman* connotes independence, competence, and seriousness of purpose as well as sexual maturity. Because these qualities in women are often seen as threatening, some people shy away from the very word, as though it were taboo, and use alternatives like *lady, girl,* and *gal* as euphemisms, especially in conversation and informal writing:

> One of the ladies who was laid off had worked on the assembly line for twenty years.

> We met several ladies from St. Louis at our hotel in Majorca.

> Did you invite all the gals in the editorial department to the party?

Despite this quasi taboo, however, *woman* has come into its own as a strong, positive term, like *man,* connoting responsible adulthood. Editor Sey Chassler used it in its cardinal sense when he ended a moving tribute to the late Margaret Mead:

> "She was a woman."

Women and Work

> "Do you talk to a working woman any differently than a housewife?" —Advertising executive

What are housewives if not working women? According to a recent study, the average housewife works 99.6 hours a week at a variety of jobs (purchasing agent, cook, cleaner, economist, chauffeur, etc.) for which the combined hourly pay scales would have earned her an annual salary of $17,351.88 in the 1978 job market.

Advertisers, along with other speakers and writers, might achieve better communication with women who are full-time homemakers if they used terms like *salaried women, wage-earning women,* or *women employed outside the home* when referring to women in the paid work force. The executive quoted above might have said

> Do you talk to a woman who works outside the home any differently than to a housewife?

It is interesting and probably significant that many women do not use the term *work* to describe their house-keeping or homemaking activities. Nor, in general, do members of their families. A woman "stays home" rather than "works at home." She "fixes dinner" rather than "works in the kitchen." In contrast, activities men tradition-ally undertake around the house are usually dignified by the name *work.* A man "works on the car" or "does his own electrical work." He may have a "workshop" in the basement.

Housewife

While the job a housewife performs is greatly undervalued, the word *housewife* itself is overworked and often used with disparaging connotations. An insurance agency advertises that its agents take the time to explain homeowners' insurance

> "in terms even a housewife can understand."

The patronizing tone of the ad would be softened if it were revised to read

> in terms the average householder can understand.

A newspaper article on the making of an animated motion picture described the vast amount of work required to produce 250,000 separate images on celluloid transparencies:

"On four floors of a Los Angeles office building, more than 150 artists did the actual animating. Two hundred housewives with steady hands did the routine work of painting the images onto cels."

Since steady hands and an aptitude for routine work are less characteristic of housewives as a class than they are of, say, watch repairers, the use of the term *housewives* here is either irrelevant or insulting: this chore is so simple even a housewife can do it. Or was the writer trying to say that after the salaried artists had completed the animation, another 200 people finished the routine painting at home on a piecework basis? If so, why not say so? If not, a better alternative would have been

Two hundred assistants selected for their steady hands did the routine work. . . .

Housewife is also usually out of place as a primary descriptive for a woman who does something newsworthy.

The counterfeit credit cards were traced to a 47-year-old Denver housewife

gives no more pertinent information than would have been conveyed by "a 47-year-old Denver woman," and it could leave some readers with the impression that a connection exists between housewifery and the use of counterfeit credit cards.

The misuse of *housewife* was epitomized a few years ago when Margaret Thatcher, who had just been elected head of the Conservative Party in Great Britain, was regularly identified in the news media as "a housewife." As it happens Thatcher, a tax lawyer and former cabinet minister, ran her own household and so was in fact a housewife. To single out that term in describing her, however, was to imply that homemaking was her chief or only skill and the primary reason the Conservatives chose her to be their leader. It is hard to imagine any circumstance in which a comparable reference would be made to a man.

Perhaps the Thatcher example should be taken as evidence of the high esteem in which the Western world holds the homemaker's job. On the contrary. About the same time Thatcher was being described as "a housewife," an American newspaper ran an article about the growing number of men who are now full-time homemakers and headed it "The Nonworkers." If in the eyes of society *housework* and *nonwork* are equated, no wonder so many women whose chosen job is to maintain a home feel obliged to describe their occupation as "just housewife."

Working Wife, Working Mother

"What is a working wife? One whose arms and legs move?"
—An editor

"Working mothers? Are there any other kind?"
—A *Little Leary* cartoon

In a series of articles entitled "Women at Work," a financial newspaper presented much well-researched factual information about women's increased participation in the labor market. But the series also reinforced some common assumptions: first, that it is always preferable in a marriage for the husband to be the breadwinner, the wife to be the homemaker and chief parent; second, that although it is acceptable for a man to hold a paid job even when he has other, adequate sources of income, a married woman who works outside the home for satisfaction rather than necessity contributes both to the unemployment of others and to growing inequities between rich and poor. Yet by omitting any consideration of the monetary value of homemaking—a figure that can be reckoned according to its replacement cost in the gross national product—the articles strengthened the widespread attitude that the unpaid work homemakers do is not an essential factor in the economy.

Whatever the merits of these assumptions, the language of the series demonstrated how deeply they have become ingrained in our thinking—and therefore in our patterns of writing and speech. This was particularly apparent in the use throughout the series of the terms *working wives* and *working mothers.*

When used to describe someone employed in a paying job, such phrases define a woman primarily in terms of her domestic role; they imply that her main responsibilities are toward something other than her employment. Though the implication is often true, it can be equally true of many men. Yet in the articles men were rarely identified as *working husbands* or *working fathers.*

> "Armed with surveys showing that working wives tend to get more help around the house from husbands . . ."

and, quoting a husband,

> " 'Working wives offer their husbands the flexibility to do what they want with their lives' "

would have been more accurately phrased

> Armed with surveys showing that wives who work outside the home tend to get more help around the house from husbands . . .

and

> Wives who bring home a paycheck offer their husbands the flexibility to do what they want with their lives.

(In the first instance housework is still assumed to be the wife's responsibility, and in the second she is still assigned a secondary, supporting role; but the language itself is no longer ambiguous.)

An eight-part series on the subject of women in the work force, especially one which drew on many interviews, could probably not be expected to avoid terms like *working wife* or *women who work* completely, and to their credit the writers of the series used many alternatives such as "women holding jobs," "women who work for pay," "job-holding wife," "working parents," and "the husband-wife working family." Phrases like "women who work at home" also indicated that work done by full-time homemakers was not being ignored. Nevertheless, the underlying assumption that women belong at home was reinforced both by the language of the writers themselves and of the people they quoted.

For example, one woman who works for a tree-spraying company was described by the writer as doing

"a man's job for equal pay,"

implying that when women compete for better-paid jobs they are invading male territory. However, a later reference in the same article used quotation marks to reflect an awareness—at least on the part of the writer and the women being interviewed—that men do not have exclusive rights to certain jobs:

"But many working women say they still have to walk softly on the job, particularly if they're doing 'man's work.' "

Women tended to be seen as wives, whereas men were called "men" more often than "husbands." In each of the following sentences, for example, *husband* (or *husbands*) would have been the appropriate parallel to *wife* (or *wives*).

" 'It can be an uncomfortable feeling for a man when his wife goes to work.' "

"There are some less obvious benefits as well that men might gain through their working wives."

" 'With a working wife, a man can refuse a transfer, quit his job or just tell his boss to go to hell. . . . A wife's job provides a lot of freedom if men are just willing to accept it.' "

And so ingrained is the image of woman as wife that she continues to be seen as a wife even when she is divorced:

"Mrs. Doe, 53, was divorced three years ago. . . . As head of a household, [she] is a member of the most underprivileged group of working wives."

Married women are seen as blameworthy in a manner not shared by men, whatever their marital, economic, or job status, or by unmarried women:

"Also disturbing are the tensions now arising between wives who work because of strict financial need and those who work because they want the status, satisfaction and adventure of carving a niche in the labor market."

Not surprisingly, wives, even when employed full time, are responsible for the smooth running of the household, as in the example already quoted and in the following:

"Local repairmen . . . get frequent requests nowadays to fix broken appliances after 4 P.M. or on Saturdays, because the customers are working wives."

Actually the reason no one is at home is

. . . because both the husband and wife have jobs,

and

"the day-time absence of employed wives"

is every bit as much

the day-time absence of husband and wife, both of whom are employed.

Even children tend to be more the mother's children than the father's. Following a description of youngsters waiting outside an elementary school before it opens in the morning, the copy reads

"Occasionally, a teacher or the principal also will come early to mind these offspring of working mothers."

Since the implication was not that these particular children are from single-parent families, but families in which both mother and father are employed, the sentence might have been phrased more equitably:

Occasionally, a teacher or the principal also will come early to mind these children whose parents both have jobs.

When the financial contribution of both spouses is the focus of attention, there is no more reason to single out women as workers (*working mothers, working wives*) than to single out men:

Most of the houses in the new development are being built by two-income families.

> A two-paycheck family usually has less trouble getting a
> mortgage.

Homemaking and Parenting

In the small percentage of one-parent families where the
parent is a man, and in two-parent families where both parents are employed, fathers increasingly perform or share
the work traditionally done by mothers. In addition, the
Internal Revenue Service lists some 200,000 men in
the United States who are full-time homemakers. Thus
the disparity in the once commonly understood meanings
of the verbs *to mother* (the social act of nurturance) and
to father (the biological act of insemination) is disappearing.
Fathering, too, has acquired the meaning "caring for or
looking after someone" previously ascribed only to
mothering, and a new word, *parenting*, is gaining acceptance.

New words come into being because enough people feel
a need for them. *Parenting* serves two purposes: it describes
the role of single parents who have to try to be both mother
and father to their children, and it de-emphasizes the ste-
reotype so frequently found in two-parent families that
only mothers are responsible for "mothering." Like the
familiar word *parenthood, parenting* conveys a sense of mutu-
ality and shared responsibility.

> Parents can help each other learn the arts of mothering
> and fathering

makes an arbitrary distinction between two prescribed
roles. A father's ability to nurture and a mother's experi-
ences in a world wider than the home are not denied when
the sentence is rephrased

> Mothers and fathers can help each other learn the art of
> parenting.

5 | Parallel Treatment

Women and *Men*

Nonparallel terminology is common in side-by-side references to the sexes, and it always seems to work one way: at women's expense. When a radio newscaster reported that

> "Three Stanford University students—two girls and a man—were abducted from a research station in Africa"

the implication was that the "girls" were less mature than the "man"—or less significant. Yet the sentence could easily have been worded

> Three Stanford University students—two women and a man—were abducted from a research station in Africa.

A newspaper reference to members of a hotel housekeeping staff suffers from the same problem:

> "Of course Miss Doe has help; in this case a large staff of men and maids."

Again, the parallel to *men* is *women,* but unless the hotel also employs children, dogs, or robots,

> . . . Miss Doe has . . . a large staff of men and women

provides even less information than the original reference. The traditional parallel to *maids* being *janitors* or *housemen,*

> . . . Miss Doe has . . . a large staff of maids and housemen

would be a step in the right direction. Better, since the sex of the employees is not germane, the writer could have used common-gender job titles (see page 28ff.) and provided additional housekeeping details in the bargain:

> Of course Miss Doe has help; in this case a large staff of room attendants, cleaners, electricians, carpenters, and plumbers.

Man and Wife

Man as a synonym for *husband* was labeled "archaic or colloquial" as long ago as 1913. If a writer were to submit an article containing the sentence

> Governor Ella Grasso was accompanied by her man of thirty-eight years and their daughter and son

an editor would undoubtedly change it to read

> Governor Ella Grasso was accompanied by her husband of thirty-eight years and their daughter and son.

Yet many writers habitually use the phrase *man and wife* when they mean "husband and wife." In commenting on the outcome of Michele Triola Marvin's lawsuit against Lee Marvin, a newspaper editorial concluded

> "The rest of the country should feel challenged at finding that the California courts pay more humane attention to a couple that once lived together outside marriage than courts elsewhere do to man and wife."

No doubt one reason the nonparallel *man and wife* persists is its traditional use in the marriage services of many churches. For example, in the ancient form provided in the Book of Common Prayer the minister says,

> "I pronounce that they are Man and Wife"

and a rubric then directs that

> "The Man and Wife kneeling, the Minister shall add this Blessing."

What many people are not aware of is that in the beginning of the same service the two people about to be married are referred to as "the Man and the Woman," and it is not until after the actual marriage has taken place that the wording changes to "Man and Wife." Symbolically, two have been made one, but also symbolically the man's status as a person remains intact whereas the woman's is changed from person to role.

In revisions of the Episcopal Church prayer book the celebrant now says,

"I pronounce that they are husband and wife,"

and it is also significant that in this version the well-known injunction

"Those whom God hath joined together let no man put asunder"

now reads

"Those whom God has joined together let no one put asunder."

(However, the traditional order of male before female, maintained throughout the service, has not been altered.)

Double Standards

Describing Women by Appearance

Emphasis on the physical characteristics of women is offensive in contexts where men are described in terms of business or other achievements:

"Engagement revealed. Lee Radziwill, 46, fine-boned younger sister of Jacqueline Onassis; and Newton Cope, 57, San Francisco hotel and real estate millionaire. . . ."

A parallel description of the principals in that news item could have read

Engagement revealed. Lee Radziwill, 46, interior decorator and younger sister of Jacqueline Onassis; and Newton Cope, 57, San Francisco hotel and real estate millionaire. . . .

Also offensive was a notice of the death of Marvella Bayh in 1979 which began

> "Marvella Bayh, vivacious blond wife of Democratic Senator Birch Bayh of Indiana and ardent fund raiser for the American Cancer Society . . ."

The subject's eight-year battle with cancer might have suggested a more dignified and appropriate beginning, such as

> Marvella Bayh, courageous wife of Democratic Senator Birch Bayh of Indiana and ardent fund raiser for the American Cancer Society . . .

or, as in the lead paragraph in another publication,

> "Marvella Bayh, special representative and long-time volunteer for the American Cancer Society and strong supporter of the Equal Rights Amendment, died of cancer on April 24 . . ."

Frequently a woman's appearance is contrasted with her capabilities as though attractiveness and competence were incompatible:

> "Dolores Doe's calm, quiet demeanor and stunning Filipino beauty belie the fact that she too hopes to finish a Ph.D. during this school year—in nuclear physics."

The disparagement implicit in the writer's astonishment is best demonstrated by imagining the parallel treatment of a man (even when the female-associated physical attribute is changed to a male-associated one):

> Juan Doe's calm, quiet demeanor and stunning Filipino physique belie the fact that he too hopes to finish a Ph.D. . . .

Trivializing

Language used to describe women's actions often implies that women behave more irrationally and emotionally than men. The writer Gena Corea cites an example of such nonparallel treatment on a network newscast. In a story about a conference on the ordination of women to the

Catholic priesthood, a reporter stated that the women broke into "bickering." Another story on the same newscast concerned a "disagreement" between Begin and Sadat over the Mideast settlement. In a letter to the network, Corea commented that "it seems women 'bicker' but men 'disagree.'"

Similarly, when a woman asserts herself on a public issue her stand is frequently trivialized by wording that would not be used of a man.

> "City Councilwoman Ruffled by Absences"

could easily have been

> City Councilwoman Critical of Absences

or

> Absenteeism Irks City Council Member.

Verbs chosen to characterize someone's actions can subtly detract from the person's effectiveness or forcefulness. Compare, for example,

> "Harriet Tubman helped slaves to escape and served as a spy"

with

> Harriet Tubman led slaves to freedom and was a spy;

or

> She serves as a lobbyist for the tobacco industry

with

> She lobbies for the tobacco industry.

Because women are traditionally perceived to be passive, they fall victim to this particular form of belittlement more often than men.

After being called "the leading lady of lexicography," Alma Graham pointed out that the phrase, though well intended, implied she was playing a role, not doing the job of a bona fide professional. Furthermore, she said, "No one would seek to flatter a man by calling him, say, 'the matinée idol of lexicography.' " As if to underscore her point, the columnist William Safire, in need of such a term for a man, once came up with "the rex of lex."

Women as Entities, Not Appendages

An entire category of nonparallel linguistic treatment involves the weight given to women's domestic relationships. In a trade journal announcement of the appointments of four men and one woman to executive posts in a large company, each man was described in terms of his previous jobs, without reference to his marital state. The woman's professional background was also given, but only after she had been identified as the widow of a well-known race car driver.

A married woman loses her identity entirely when she and her husband are lumped under one name—his. A newsphoto showing two women and two men, all of them huddling under a large plastic sheet as they watch a baseball game in the rain, is captioned:

> "Joe Poe (far right) and Ron Doe (beside him) and their wives did not let the rain chase them to cover."

The caption could easily have read:

> Four fans who did not let the rain chase them to cover were (left to right) Rose Doe, June Poe, Ron Doe, and Joe Poe.

One reason women tend to be identified as somebody's wife is the social custom, which goes back only to the nineteenth century, of calling a married woman by her husband's full name, prefixed by "Mrs." (see **The Social Titles** *Mrs., Miss,* **and** *Ms.,* page 100). Some women, among them Mrs. Humphry Ward, the writer and antisuffragist, and Mrs. H. H. A. Beach, the composer, even insisted on being known professionally by their husbands' names rather than their own. And their influence lingers. Today one would expect to read

Joan A. Mondale, art consultant and author of *Politics in Art,*

but as recently as 1972, when that book for children was published, a newspaper item began

"Mrs. Walter F. Mondale, wife of the Democratic Senator from Minnesota, has managed to get her first book published, in spite of . . ."

The accompanying picture was captioned "Mrs. Walter F. Mondale," and nowhere in the story did the name of the author herself appear.

Even when women are better known than their husbands, some writers must sense the Mesdames Ward and Beach looking over their shoulders. The sentence

Mrs. Louis Francis, whose husband is a career foreign service officer, has written her third best-selling novel

gets Louis in all right. But does he belong? If a woman's husband's career has a bearing on a story about her, he might be mentioned early on:

Martha Francis has written her third best seller. The novelist, whose husband, Louis Francis, is a foreign service officer, has lived in the Far East for many years, and her tightly plotted stories capture . . .

But even under those circumstances, Louis, if mentioned at all, probably belongs in the last paragraph rather than the first.

Incidental information about children and grandchildren is also often prominently included in news of women, as though the number of her offspring was the major definer of a woman's life and an indicator of her intellectual or executive competence:

"Mother of 5
To Represent
State Students

"A Milford mother of five was named to the state Board of Higher Education Monday. . . ."

Was she appointed because anyone with five children is presumed to understand the problems of students? No. As later paragraphs establish, the appointment was made because the woman was herself a part-time student active in several statewide student groups. A more straightforward and informative approach might have been

> Student Named
> To State Board
> Of Education
>
> A Milford woman active in student affairs was named to the state Board of Higher Education. . . .

Another newspaper story, this one reporting on a four-year study of prostitution, identified the sociologist who did the study by her university affiliation, but the next reference to her began

> "Doe, a 35-year-old mother of two who teaches a course in deviant behavior . . ."

Was Doe's motherhood mentioned to provide a note of respectability? Or, on the contrary, was there an implied question: what is a *mother* doing studying deviant behavior? Whatever the reason, a similar article about a man would almost certainly omit reference to his fatherhood:

> Roe, 35, who teaches a course in deviant behavior . . .

or would include it only with other biographical material.

Sometimes it seems that when women are identified as wives, mothers, and grandmothers, especially in contexts where men are not identified in similar ways, the message is intended to be that women do things for love, men for profit:

> "Two of the 1,000 inventions patented this week are aimed at improving the health and safety of babies. One is an alarm belt to monitor an infant's condition and reduce crib fatalities. The other, offered by a grandmother, is a collapsible outdoor shelter. . . ."

The second paragraph of this newspaper story named the two people (they were men) who had invented the monitor and mentioned their jobs, though not their marital state or relationship to babies. After giving the name and occupation of the inventor of the outdoor shelter, however, the story went on to give her husband's name and occupation and the additional information that she was the mother of three children and the grandmother of two. If this information was included because it was supposed to have a bearing on the invention of a device to protect babies, would not the parenthood and grandparenthood of the two other inventors have been equally apropos?

On some occasions information about a person's children, grandchildren, and spouse is relevant and of genuine interest. In deciding whether and how to refer to a woman's family relationships, the best test is to ask oneself, "Would I write it this way if the subject were a man?" The answer is clear in the case of the following headline and lead paragraph of a wire service news story which has been rewritten to change the sex of the subject, and sex-related words, but nothing else:

> "Coast Grandpa, 56,
> Drives Heavy Truck
> "Fulfilling his lifelong dream, John Doe, a 56-year-old grandfather of eight, has begun driving a 76,000-pound truck and double trailer for a freight company full time."

Order

The convention of placing males first whenever reference is made to people of both sexes is a deeply embedded habit in writing and speech. It is also a habit that can be broken by conscious effort. A news story by science writer Lawrence K. Altman began

> "A West German wife-husband team of doctors has invented a device that promises to reduce significantly the number of common birth defects. . . ."

and Altman later named the team as

> "Dr. Renate Huch and Dr. Albert Huch of the University of Marburg."

But despite the refreshing reversal of the usual order, the caption under the accompanying photograph followed the old pattern. Although Renate Huch stands to the viewer's left and her husband to the right, the caption reads

> "Dr. Albert Huch and wife, Renate, at Marburg hospital."

Since English-speaking people are accustomed to reading pictures as we read type, from left to right, why did the caption writer not opt for

> Dr. Renate Huch and Dr. Albert Huch at Marburg hospital

or, if brevity was essential,

> Drs. Renate and Albert Huch at Marburg hospital.

People come up with all sorts of reasons why in word pairs males almost always come first: "men and women," "male and female," "his and hers," "boys and girls," "guys and dolls," etc. Some linguists theorize that it is easier to say a single-syllable word like *men* than a two-syllable word like *women*, and that we tend to put the single syllable first as a result. Another theory is that the order has something to do with prosodic patterns: since "men and women" and "male and female" scan as two trochees, they trip more lightly off the tongue than they would if reversed to scan as a trochee and an iamb. Neither theory accounts for "husbands and wives" or such other familiar phrases as "coffee and cake," "needle and thread," "hammer and tongs," "fathers and sons," or—to get to the root of the matter—"Adam and Eve."

It seems clear that the convention of male precedence in English followed the same pattern as the arrogation to males of the Old English word *man* and the grammarians' pronouncement that *he* is generic. To insure observance of the convention, an early grammarian, Thomas Wilson, formulated the following "rule," published in 1553:

> Some will set the Carte before the horse, as thus. My mother and my father are both at home, even as thoughe the good man of the house ware no breaches, or that the graye Mare were the better horse. And what thoughe it often so happeneth (God wotte the more pitte) yet in speaking at the leaste, let us kepe a natural order, and set the man before the woman for maners Sake.

Those who have no stake in maintaining the so-called natural order of the sexes do not set one before the other as a matter of rule; they allow, instead, for variations that come naturally:

> "Search until you find the therapist who believes as much as you do that recovery *is* possible, and then cherish her or him as you would your most precious possession."

> "Gentlemen and ladies, this is our last class before the spring break."

> "The Point Reyes Light . . . a 16-page weekly with a circulation of 2,700 is put out by Catherine and David Mitchell, the owners, and one full-time reporter."

Names and Titles

Women are frequently referred to by their first names in circumstances where men are called by their last names. The impression created, intentionally or not, is that women merit less respect, less serious consideration, or perhaps more paternalistic indulgence than men. When in 1979 Kentucky's lieutenant governor, Thelma Stovall, had differences with then governor Julian Carroll, a news magazine report contained this passage:

> "A popular tax cut was not the only thing on Thelma's mind. As she well knew, her desire to shake things up while the boss is away had made her a political heroine. She is now one of the favorites in this year's race to succeed Carroll. . . ."

The story referred to the lieutenant governor as "Thelma" six times, whereas it called the governor "Carroll," "Governor Carroll," or "the Governor"—never "Julian." Since parallel terms were available, for example,

> A popular tax cut was not the only thing on Stovall's mind,

the nonparallel use of the lieutenant governor's first name was an editorial choice and made an editorial statement.

The problem of names may be a little more difficult when the subjects have the same surname, as in the following:

> "Quietly but firmly, Carter maintained his commitment to nuclear development. At the height of the crisis, he visited Three Mile Island with Rosalynn, in part to demonstrate that there was little risk."

Rewritten, Rosalynn Carter can be seen as a self-directed, active participant in the visit rather than as someone brought along to bolster the message that there was little nuclear risk:

> Quietly but firmly, the President maintained his commitment to nuclear development. At the height of the crisis he and Rosalynn Carter visited Three Mile Island, in part to demonstrate that there was little risk.

First-naming men who are close to prominent women is no less belittling, as another quote about Margaret Thatcher demonstrates:

> "Normally, Thatcher is up at 6:30 A.M. to cook Denis' breakfast and do the shopping before heading off for Parliament"

makes Denis Thatcher, a man in his sixties, sound like a child. Unless Margaret Thatcher herself skips breakfast, the sentence could have read:

> Normally, Thatcher is up at 6:30 A.M. to cook breakfast and do the shopping. . . .

The deeply ingrained custom of identifying women by social titles sometimes results in subtle distinctions.

Governor Carey and Mrs. Grasso agreed to appoint a joint commission

or

Carey and Mrs. Grasso agreed to appoint a joint commission

downgrade Connecticut's chief executive. Since the governors acted as equals, those who agreed are

Carey and Grasso

or

Mr. Carey and Mrs. Grasso [Governor Grasso does not use Ms.]

or

Governor Carey and Governor Grasso.

The same principle applies in the case of academic or professional titles. A magazine article about a pharmacologist included the information that his wife is a physiologist. Both have Ph.D.s and hold academic appointments. But a picture accompanying the article was captioned:

"Dr. and Mrs. Doe at home with their two-year-old Irish setter, Jennie."

If the article had been primarily about a woman, would the caption have read "Dr. and Mr. Doe . . ." or "Mr. and Dr. Doe . . ."? One assumes not.

The Drs. Doe at home with their two-year-old Irish setter, Jennie

would have been fine.

When a wife and husband work together as a professional team their identity is in both their names. Although

Mr. and Mrs. Will Durant

may be an accepted way to address a formal wedding announcement, the authors of *The Age of Napoleon* are

Will and Ariel Durant.

If a writer does not bother to give the first name of a woman who has taken her husband's surname on marriage, her identity can be obscured or even lost.

> "[A] single citizen can still count—like Mrs. Klussman, who saved the San Francisco cable car in the 40s, and Dr. A. J. Haagen-Smit, the first man to prove that smog is not a byproduct of nature but is chemically created in the atmosphere. . . ."

Who was "Mrs. Klussman," and how can one find out more about her? It would have taken only a little effort for the writer to discover her full name and so give parallel credit to two noteworthy activists:

> . . . like Friedel Klussman, who saved the San Francisco cable car . . .

A familiar journalistic practice in reports of accidents, arrests, and other unhappy events is exemplified by

> Smith was hospitalized with leg fractures, and the Jones woman was treated for minor injuries and released.

The usage may stem from an old-fashioned reluctance to call a woman by her last name alone, but the effect is demeaning. Reference is sometimes made also to "the Jones girl," "the Jones boy," even "the Jones dog," but one would rarely, if ever, read that

> Smith was hospitalized with leg fractures, and the Jones man was treated for minor injuries and released.

Women in the arts and professions have for years used their own names (that is, a family name, a previously held surname, or an adopted name) rather than a husband's surname. Today more women than ever before are making the same choice. Yet writers often seem reluctant to respect their wishes, with such awkward results as

> "These are sentiments that Martin Ritt, the director, and Irving Ravetch and Harriet Frank Jr. (Mrs. Ravetch), his screenwriters, understand and fervently evoke in their stirring new film. . . ."

and later in the same review

> "Mr. Ritt and the Ravetches, who've been collaborating on films since . . ."

In addition to being a collaborator with her husband on screenplays, Harriet Frank Jr. is an established writer and novelist. Professionally she is neither "Mrs. Ravetch" nor one of "the Ravetches." If the film critic quoted above thought it was essential to mention the Frank-Ravetch conjugal relationship, the earlier sentence might have begun

> These are the sentiments that Martin Ritt, the director, and the husband-and-wife screenwriting team of Irving Ravetch and Harriet Frank Jr. understand and fervently evoke in their stirring new film. . . .

and the second might have read

> Mr. Ritt, Mr. Ravetch, and Ms. Frank have been collaborating on films since . . .

Famous women in sports seem to have an even harder time holding onto their own names than do women in the arts. After her marriage, Yvonne Goolagong expressed her wish to be known professionally by that name rather than as Yvonne Cawley or Mrs. Cawley, but her preference is frequently ignored. When Chris Evert married, her preference was to be called Chris Evert Lloyd, but she has become to most reporters, and so to the public, Mrs. Lloyd. Even those who follow tennis casually become accustomed to these apparent newcomers, but in the process, and against their will, women are manipulated. (See also **Sports Reporting,** beginning on page 59, especially page 61.)

How serious the consequences of an arbitrary name change can be is illustrated by the case of a woman in politics who married during an election campaign. Because some newspapers then insisted on referring to her by her husband's name rather than the one familiar to her constituents, she was forced to go to court to protect her right to be called by the name of her choice.

The Social Titles *Mrs.*, *Miss*, and *Ms.*

Mrs., *Miss*, and *Ms.* are all abbreviations for the now-outdated social title *Mistress*. In the seventeenth and eighteenth centuries the oldest of the three, *Mrs.*, was commonly used before the family name (or given and family name) of an adult woman, whether she was single or married. *Miss* as a social title was limited to female children (although as a noun it had the second meaning, as did *mistress*, of "concubine" or "prostitute").

Sometime in the late eighteenth century the social title *Miss* began to be used to distinguish single women from married women, and in the nineteenth century the custom developed of prefixing *Mrs.* to a man's first and last names to identify his wife. In this way, over a period of years, a system evolved by which women, unlike men, were designated "single," "married," "divorced." In the heyday of naming etiquette, for example, Miss Beatrice Hansen became Mrs. Joseph O'Malley when she and Joseph O'Malley were married, and she became Mrs. Hansen O'Malley (or, less formally, Mrs. Beatrice O'Malley) if they were divorced.

The dissatisfaction of many women with this labeling system led eventually to the use of *Ms.*, which first appeared in secretarial handbooks in the 1940s as a title analogous to *Mr.* The American Heritage Dictionary defines *Ms.* as "A title of courtesy used before a woman's surname or before her given name and surname, without regard to her marital status," and it gives the plural as *Mses.* or *Mss.* Most current dictionaries contain similar definitions, and the usage is recognized by many influential publications, including the *Congressional Record*.

Misunderstanding of the purpose of *Ms.* has occasionally resulted in uses like

Ms. Walter Klein is chairwoman of the committee.

If circumstances call for an honorific, the form would be
Ms. Dorothy Klein.

Although the *Mrs./Miss* distinction is not a reliable indicator of whether or not a woman is married (she may continue to use *Miss* after marriage or, if divorced, may continue to use the title *Mrs.*), many people, including many
women, feel strongly that these older titles should be retained, as the following verse attests:

> In typing *Ms.* for *Mrs.*
> Your Smith Corona slipped.
> I am a wife and mother
> And not a manuscript.

Others do not care. Still others are strongly committed
to *Ms.* or would prefer no title at all. As another versifier
put it:

> When you call me *Miss* or *Mrs.*
> You invade my private life,
> For it's not the public's business
> If I am, or was, a wife.

Because many people do feel strongly about social titles,
the obvious and courteous solution for anyone writing
about a particular woman is to follow her preference. (See
Salutations in Letters, page 102, for a discussion of writing
to women.) If the writer does not know or cannot guess
what that preference is, the simplest way out is to use
no title in the first reference and her last name without
title thereafter:

> Dorothy Klein is chairwoman of the committee. Yesterday
> Klein said . . .

A growing trend is to drop social titles entirely for both
women and men. In fact the absence of a social title, as
in this example from an author's preface, sometimes becomes a mark of distinction:

> "I wish to thank my colleagues Jane Doe and John Roe
> who read the manuscript and gave me many valuable sug-
> gestions, and Mrs. Mary Poe whose patience in deciphering

> my handwriting and typing the many drafts required to finish this work was infinite."

Writers who must follow the established style of a particular publication may have no choice in the use of titles. The *New York Times Manual of Style and Usage,* for example, mandates that second references in stories in the *Times* include either *Mr., Mrs.,* or *Miss.* The honorific *Ms.,* the manual states, is to be used "only in quoted matter, in letters to the editor and, in news articles, in passages discussing the term itself." In a personal letter commenting on the paper's policy, a member of the *Times* staff wrote, "You can imagine how difficult it is to establish rapport with feminists when you must first establish their marital status during the interview."

Salutations in Letters

Year after year the popular and authoritative *World Almanac* carried the following note under the heading "Forms of Address":

> "The salutation Dear Sir is always permissible when addressing a person not known to the writer."

In the 1979 edition the note changed:

> "The salutation Dear Sir or Dear Madam is always permissible when addressing a person not known to the writer."

A victory for common sense. Addressing a letter "Dear Sir or Dear Madam" is cumbersome, however, and retains the traditional order.

> Dear Madam or Sir

has the advantage of brevity. The order is alphabetical, but anyone who likes to play the odds is free, of course, to indulge their hunches either way.

"Gentlemen," the usual plural of the traditional "Dear Sir" salutation, lends itself comfortably to the more inclusive

Gentlemen and Ladies.

As in the previous example, the alphabetical order can be reversed without strain. Also favored by some is the sex-neutral variation

Gentlepeople.

A more conventional solution in addressing an unknown person or group of people is to use the title of the job or group:

Dear Credit Manager

Dear Director of Admissions

Dear Members of the Gaming Commission (*or* Dear Commissioners).

This salutation also works when writing to a company:

Dear Grumble Brothers

Dear North Pole Airlines.

A form letter addressed to individuals in a category often suggests its own salutation:

Dear Homeowner

Dear Friend of the Library.

A school that sends an occasional newsletter to students' homes using the salutation

Dear Mother

might improve communication with many of its readers by using

Dear Parent or Guardian.

Anyone who feels that "dear" is unduly affectionate has the alternative either of omitting any salutation, instead going from the inside address directly to the body of the letter, or of framing the letter as a memo:

To the Credit Manager, Grumble Brothers

To the President, North Pole Airlines.

When the person addressed is known to the writer the degree of formality in the salutation depends, of course, on their relationship. If the addressee is a woman and the writer is uncertain which, if any, social title she prefers (see **The Social Titles** *Mrs.*, *Miss*, **and** *Ms.*, page 100), addressing her by her first and last names is always acceptable:

> Dear Catherine Castille.

A professional or academic title, if she has one, takes precedence over a social title:

> Dear Dr. Castille
> Dear Professor Castille
> Dear Senator Castille.

6 | A Few More Words

Alumnae, Alumni

The plural of the feminine-gender word *alumna* is *alumnae;* the plural of the masculine-gender word *alumnus* is *alumni.* These atypical English words, taken over from classical Latin without any change in spelling, have no common-gender forms.

Predictably, men who graduate from an institution that formerly enrolled only women object to being called "alumnae," whereas women who graduate from any institution attended by men are expected to acquiesce in being called "alumni." When a seventy-year-old school of nursing graduated its first male student a few years ago, the Alumnae Association immediately changed its name to Alumni Association.

Vassar was more respectful of its own long tradition as a women's college when in 1969 its Alumnae Association voted to become the Alumnae and Alumni of Vassar College. The following year, however, the association's bylaws were further amended to change all nonspecific uses of *alumnae* to *alumni,* "it being understood that the word 'alumni' is both masculine and feminine."

Use of the passive verb form begs the important question, *who* understands that *alumni* is both masculine and feminine? Many women who went to schools and colleges that later became coeducational neither understand nor accept that assumption. Nor did the people who spoke Latin as their native tongue. On the contrary, Roman law-makers included both the masculine- and feminine-gender forms of all personal nouns and pronouns in the wording of certain laws to make explicit that they applied to both women and men.

Women who object to being called "alumni" may be challenged on the grounds that words frequently change their meanings, and this one can presumably expand to become an umbrella term for both sexes. Perhaps it can, if it is forced, but it would be one more case of subsuming women under "generic" terms that are really masculine-gender words. When men demur at being called "alum-nae," their sensibilities are respected, and women deserve the same courtesy.

Alternatives to the false generic *alumni* are

  alumnae and alumni (or the other way around)
and
  alumnae/i (or the other way around).

An individual woman is an *alumna,* just as a woman who holds the rank of retired professor is a *professor emerita.*

Blond/Blonde and Similar Imports

When English took over the masculine-gender French words *blond* and *brunet,* it also annexed their feminine-gen-der counterparts *blonde* and *brunette* and acquired in the process special, nonstandard English nouns to use of fe-males: "He is a blond. She is a blonde."

Unlike *alumnus* and *alumna,* where sex-differentiated end-ings from Latin mark both terms, the seemingly innocuous difference between *blond* and *blonde* becomes in English the difference between the standard (male) and the devia-tion (female). Why not *blond* for both women and men?

Similar words from the French that still have nonstan-dard (for English) feminine-gender endings are *fiancé/fian-cée* and *divorcé/divorcée.* Although English dictionaries define both forms of *fiancé*, it is significant that many define only the feminine-gender form *divorcée*, indicating our society's predilection for labeling a woman's marital circumstances more frequently than a man's.

We are creatures of habit, of course, but in the interest of simplicity and logic the common-gender forms *blond*, *brunet*, *fiancé*, and *divorcé* would seem to suffice for everybody.

Coed

This word entered American English around the turn of the century as derisive slang. It exemplified the scorn and hostility directed at women who chose to invade male bastions of higher learning at a time when many women's colleges were little more than finishing schools. Even after the idea of higher education for women became widely accepted, *coed* as a noun retained a connotation of frivolity that continues to impair the image of women as serious students.

The word is rarely used as a noun in a strictly academic context. To speak of a Rhodes scholar as a "coed," for example, would belittle both the individual and the award, and associating the term with physical descriptions, as in

the slim dark coed

or

a bevy of beautiful coeds

contributes to its trivializing effect. *Coed* is particularly out of place when used of women who are victims of crime or violence, as the distinguished anchor of a network television news program habitually uses the word:

"The defendant is being tried for the murder of two coeds."

"The twenty-year-old coed was kidnapped and buried alive."

The use of *coed* is often justified on the grounds that it gives more information than either *woman* alone (which omits the person's status as a student) or *student* (which omits the person's sex). True. But in the examples above the speaker could easily have used both. If a male were the subject, would anyone cavil at having to use extra words to explain either that he was also a student or that the student referred to was male?

As an abbreviation for *coeducational,* the adjective *coed* is a useful one to describe an institution or program for students of both sexes:

> Clarke College, founded as a women's college in 1843, is now coed.

But unless it is also used evenhandedly of males and females, *coed* as a noun will continue to be still another term that defines women as aberrations.

Fellow

Fellow went through a period when it was used primarily of males, perhaps because the common compound *fellowman* suffered the same narrowing of meaning as *man* itself. During its early history (*fellow* dates from Old English) the word was not so restricted. It meant, according to the Oxford English Dictionary, "a partner, colleague, co-worker." It was also used in the sense of "companion" or "spouse." In Shakespeare's *The Tempest,* Miranda says,

> "I am your wife, if you will marry me . . . to be your fellow . . ."

Since *fellowship* and *fellow worker* have never been limited to one sex, and today the many women who receive academic fellowships are called "fellows," all forms of the word—with the exception of *fellowman*—can be used sex-inclusively.

The problem with *fellowman* comes not from *fellow* but from the protean term *man,* which is sometimes intended to include everyone, sometimes to include males only (see Chapter 1). This ambiguity often surfaces in election years when those running for office become more careful than usual about their language. Then, for example,

> I would like to be of service to my fellowman

is apt to be corrected in mid-sentence to

> —that is, to my fellow citizens.

"Feminine" Suffixes

Most English agent-nouns—words like *author, farmer, narrator,* etc., which signify the performer of an action—have common gender and so can be used specifically of a person of either sex. When French or Latin feminine-gender suffixes like *-ess* and *-trix* are attached to these words to designate women, even if the addition is intended as a courtesy, the basic form acquires a predominantly masculine sense with the unavoidable implication that the feminine-gender form represents a substandard variation.

Readers would be shocked to come upon the sentence

> The museum is showing the works of a sculptor and a black sculptor.

Yet statements like the following are widely accepted:

> The museum is showing the works of a sculptor and a sculptress.

Just as in Western societies the absence of color identification for one of two sculptors in the first example implies that whiteness is the standard, so the absence of sex identification for one of two sculptors in the second implies that maleness is the standard. The sentence can simply read

> The museum is showing the works of two sculptors.

-Ess

The terms *princess, duchess,* and *countess* are little changed from the French versions of those words that entered English as a result of the Norman Conquest in the eleventh century, and they will probably be with us as long as titles of nobility are applicable. Common English words with -*ess* endings, like *actress, waitress, patroness,* and *stewardess,* however, are more recent inventions and carry the implication of "nonstandard," as can be seen from the history of the term *actress.*

When women first began to act on the English stage in the seventeenth century, *actor* (in the sense of a theatrical player) had been in use for about seventy-five years, and women, too, were initially called "actors." A few decades later, *actress* was coined to distinguish females in the acting profession from males, but no comparable new term was introduced to designate the latter. Thus *actor* regained a specific masculine sense and at the same time—as in "actors' guild"—continued to be used as the generic term covering both sexes. Today it is noteworthy that many women in the theater and films are beginning to take back the term *actor,* using it in reference to themselves and other women.

Some -*ess* endings present problems for equal opportunity employers. For example, a newspaper help-wanted column headed "Male and Female" includes an ad beginning

"Waitresses needed both full and parttime . . ."

Since men are unlikely to apply for jobs called "waitress" (and women are not apt to apply at this time for jobs with the male-associated label "waiter") one solution might be to use a term like *server* or *table server* until the standard, *waiter,* can be reinstated as a common-gender noun. (Another possibility is to adopt a new but recognizable term, as one Boston restaurant has done. A note on its menu says "Ask your waitron about today's special.")

Hostess, used in the sense of a person who greets people in a restaurant and leads them to a table, poses a similar difficulty. Women who host television shows are usually called "hosts," not "hostesses," a precedent that suggests the same term might be used for restaurant employees of both sexes who greet patrons (of both sexes, of course).

Several airlines have dropped the *stewardess/steward* distinction in favor of the common-gender *flight attendant.*

Attached to proper nouns, *-ess* endings are especially offensive. Fortunately *Negress, Jewess, Quakeress,* etc., are almost defunct today (and it is interesting to note in passing that no one ever came up with *whitess, WASPess,* or *Protestantess).*

-Ette

Junior Chamber of Commerce organizations in some cities welcome members of both sexes, but the national Jaycees maintain a policy of excluding women from full membership. Instead, women are relegated to auxiliary organizations called, predictably, the Jaycee-ettes. The *-ette* suffix in English also signifies imitation, as in *leatherette,* and small size, as in *kitchenette.* The upshot is that terms like *farmerette, majorette, Redskinette,* etc., effectively define females as part of a sideshow.

-Trix

The Latin feminine-gender suffix *-trix* sounds pretentious in modern English when tacked onto common-gender personal nouns. The archaic *executrix* is still used in legal documents, but discerning writers and speakers avoid such affectations as *narratrix, aviatrix,* and *administratrix,* and there is no reason *executrix* cannot be added to that list.

Despite a long-term trend toward dropping "feminine" endings, these suffixes began to reappear in the 1970s, suggesting a backlash (conscious or otherwise) to the women's movement. An article in a prestigious weekly magazine identifies Gloria Steinem as an "editress"; a noted filmmaker describes Sylvia Plath as a "poetess"; and many writers and commentators call women like Elizabeth Cady Stanton and Susan B. Anthony "suffragettes" (q.v.).

It is especially revealing that women ordained to the Episcopal priesthood are sometimes referred to as "priestesses" by those who oppose women's ordination. The Episcopal Church in the United States does not have "priestesses"; it has "priests," an order now open to people of both sexes.

For different reasons, *Goddess* and *Creatrix* have recently seen increased usage among people who want to call attention to the once widespread worship of a supreme deity conceived of as female. For others, however, the use of such terms implies that *God* and *Creator* refer to a male deity, a concept most thoughtful religious people reject as idolatrous.

Of all the techniques for avoiding linguistic sexism, none is simpler than using the same agent-nouns for both sexes. Neither sex has a monopoly on jobs or the designations that go with them—except, as attorney Florynce Kennedy has pointed out, in the case of wet nurses and sperm donors.

Heroine

Although *heroine* has a long, honorable history going back to the Greek *heroine* (counterpart of the masculine-gender *heros*), its use today involves the same problem presented by other English words used specifically of females when no comparable masculine-gender term exists. Moreover the suffix *-ine*, which has the sense of "of" or "pertaining to," suggests relationship to something rather than a thing in itself. It occurs in adjectives like *alpine, canine,* and *masculine,* and in a number of derivative names like *Pauline, Ernestine,* and *Josephine.*

Anyone who performs a heroic deed is a hero, regardless of their sex. When four young women received awards recently for aiding an elderly mugging victim and capturing her assailant, the New York City police commissioner said to them,

"Even among heroes, you folks stand out."

Had he used the word *heroines* instead, his comment would have been condescending. By the same token, a reference to Belgian patriot Gabrielle Petit (1893–1916) as a

"spy and national heroine"

would have been stronger if *hero* had been used in place of the sex-limited term.

The difference between using *hero* for both sexes and *man* for both sexes is a practical one. The meaning of

> Joan of Arc was a hero

is clear and comprehensive; modern English renders meaningless a statement like

> Joan of Arc was a brave man.

Maiden

This poetic term evokes the image of a young woman, usually beautiful, possibly dressed in Elizabethan costume, perhaps curtsying or blushing or fainting, and nearly always in need of a male protector. As a noun, *maiden* has had several other meanings, including an eighteenth-century washing machine and a guillotinelike instrument used in Scotland for beheading people in the sixteenth and seventeenth centuries.

In its most common use today, as an adjective, the word expresses, and none too subtly, the cultural view that marriage is a woman's prime destiny. *Maiden* is defined as "unmarried" (said only of women), "virgin," "fresh," "unused," and "intact," as well as "inexperienced" and "untried." To call a woman a "maiden lady" or a "maiden aunt" may seem less pejorative than calling her an "old maid," but it reflects much the same assumption that leads to calling a racehorse of either sex which has never won a race a "maiden horse." The Oxford English Dictionary's long entry on the figurative uses of *maiden* begins with the definition "That has yielded no results." In this sense the word designates a court session at which no cases are tried and a period in a cricket game in which no runs are scored, along with metal that has never been worked and soil that has never been ploughed.

Although the analogies are less judgmental when *maiden* is used to mean "first" or "earliest," as in a ship's "maiden voyage" or a new legislator's "maiden speech" in the legislature, the other connotations of the word are enough to vitiate its meaning when applied to present-day women. Even the patriarchal idea that a woman has a "maiden name" is losing standing: many people now prefer the alternative expression "birth name," which also appears in the civil codes of several states that have statutes concerning the use or restoration of a woman's "birth name or former name."

Master

Clifton Fadiman, reviewing a novel by Helen MacInness, wrote:

> "In her field she is a master. In fact she may well be *the* master."

Once the masculine-gender counterpart of *mistress, master* is no longer limited to males except in the rare instances where it is still used as a courtesy title for young boys.

As a verb ("She mastered calculus and trigonometry") and an adjective ("She is a master landscape architect"), the word has long since outgrown its masculine-gender origins. Nevertheless, some writers, unlike Clifton Fadiman in the example above, hesitate to use it as a noun when referring to a woman. A reviewer who wrote of a book by Doris Lessing,

> "This superb anthology of short stories by a current master (mistress?) of the genre . . ."

not only distracted the reader's attention foolishly but deprecated Lessing's abilities. Although *mistress* retains a sense of authority in some of its definitions (as in "headmistress of a school"), it has acquired no associations with exceptional skill or achievement. Having few uses not better served by other terms, it appears to be moving toward obsolescence and is an unlikely candidate for rehabilitation.

Until a few years ago the post of "master" of a residential college at Yale University was always filled by a male faculty member. If the wife of a master also lived at the college and shared his duties, she was called the "mistress" of the college. In the early 1970s the university began to appoint women to the post of master, and for a time there was confusion over the designation. By the end of the decade, however, Yale seemed to have taken a firm stand and was announcing the appointments of female as well as male faculty members to the post of master.

The presence of *master* in many combinations like *masterful, mastery, masterpiece,* and *mastermind* assures its continuance as a useful sex-neutral term.

Midwife

Another old word whose meaning has expanded is *midwife*, now an accepted designation for a person of either sex trained to assist at a birth. Although it was occasionally applied to male practitioners in the eighteenth century, the word as well as the practice lost status with the rise of modern medicine when midwifery was disparaged and even outlawed in most parts of the United States. In the past decade, however, the midwife has made a dramatic comeback as a highly trained specialist. Today nursing school programs in nurse-midwifery actively recruit members of both sexes, and more than twenty-five hundred certified nurse-midwives, including some two hundred men, are now practicing in this country.

Midwife initially meant "a woman" (the original meaning of *wife*) "with" *(mid)* another woman giving birth. Jokes have been made about sex-neutralizing the word to *midspouse*, but just as a person who practices midwifery does not have to be a wife in the modern sense of "married woman," so that person does not have to be a wife in the ancient sense of "woman." Like *master, midwife* has become a common-gender word. It has also acquired the additional meaning of "one that helps to produce or bring forth something." Shakespeare used it as a noun in *Richard II,*

"thou art the midwife of my woe"

and it is sometimes used as a verb, as in

> "probably the first time in history that a bank midwived a successful biographical novel."

This figurative meaning of *midwife* is reinforced by another word, the adjective *maieutic,* which has to do with the Socratic method of eliciting and clarifying ideas, and which comes from the Greek *maieuesthai,* "to act as midwife."

Old Wives' Tale

An "old wife," according to Webster's Third New International Dictionary, is "a prattling old woman: GOSSIP." That dictionary does not define *old wives' tale,* but others do. Its predecessor, Webster's Second, gives the meaning as "A tale, or bit of lore, or a notion, esp. a superstitious traditional notion, characteristic of old women," and the American Heritage Dictionary provides "A bit of superstitious folklore."

Like old men, old women can be garrulous and given to gossip and superstition. But they can also be sages, the possessors of great wisdom about human nature and human ills and their cures. It is this quality of wisdom that the phrase *old wives' tale,* as it has typically been used over some four hundred years, ignores. Compare, for example, a verse translated in the King James Version of the Bible as

> "But refuse profane and old wives' fables . . ."

with the translation in the Revised Standard Version (1946), which is more faithful to the Greek original:

> "Have nothing to do with godless and silly myths. . . ."

At a time when many women are insisting on a return to some of the humane techniques of midwifery which were lost when obstetrics became largely a male preserve, the following use, cited by the unabridged Random House Dictionary, is particularly ironic:

> "Modern medicine has dispelled many old wives' tales about childbearing."

Interestingly, the Anglo-Saxon meaning of *wife* (i.e., "woman") is preserved in the phrase *old wives' tale*. Rather than abandon it, speakers and writers might well use *old wives' tale* to evoke the kind of valuable knowledge and insights women have traditionally passed along to one another from generation to generation.

Such a use is suggested by the following account. In 1775 the British physician William Withering heard about a folk remedy for the treatment of dropsy, an accumulation of fluid in the body associated with heart disease. "I was told that it had long been kept a secret by an old woman in Shropshire, who had sometimes made cures after the more regular practitioners had failed," Dr. Withering wrote. He persuaded the woman, identified only as a "Mrs. Hutton," to tell him her remedy, which, it turned out, was made from the leaves of the foxglove plant *Digitalis purpurea*. Using foxglove infusions on his own patients, Dr. Withering experimented with different dosages and eventually published his findings in 1785. Thus the discovery of digitalis was in reality the transfer of an old wives' tale into the body of information known to medical science.

Person

This useful word has been much reviled by people who think sexism in language is a trivial issue. Professor Jacques Barzun, writing about what he calls "the *person* binge of today," poses the question, "Who does not feel that in its most general sense, which asserts anonymity, the word is disagreeably hoity-toity: 'There is a person at the door'?" Lots of people, apparently, for although Professor Barzun rigs his example ("There's someone at the door" would be more natural), it is in the sense of "someone," "a human being who may be of either sex," that the term is most widely used today. As for precedent, nobody has complained that *person* is disagreeably hoity-toity in the United States Constitution where it is used repeatedly in reference to the President, Vice President, Senators, and Representatives, as well as to the citizenry: ". . . nor shall any state deprive any person of life, liberty, or property . . ."

Unlike "generic" *man*, *person* clearly conveys common gender—which is why it is a frequent choice today to replace traditional *man* terms. A camping equipment store advertises

"Two-person Timberline Tents."

A form letter from the U.S. Small Business Administration describing government contract opportunities begins

"Dear Small Businessperson."

Columnist Nicholas Von Hoffman comments on the discomfort experienced by public figures whose relatives write books or go on talk shows in order

"to cash in on their famous kinsperson."

And the American Lutheran Church, like a number of other religious bodies, has revised its official documents to employ common-gender terms such as *layperson* in place of *layman*.

One reason *person* is a special target of ridicule may be that it is frequently used unnecessarily and therefore awkwardly:

"ABC College . . . recently released the names of students who have been placed on the Dean's List. One of the persons named to the list is . . ."

could be

. . . One of those named to the list is . . .

Similarly,

"I married a person who believes that we have a partnership"

could be

I married someone who believes we have a partnership

or, since the speaker was a woman,

I married a man who believes we have a partnership.

Perhaps because of its association with efforts to achieve equality of the sexes, *person* is sometimes misunderstood (or misinterpreted) to mean "woman." When terms like *chairman* and *spokesman* are used for men while *chairperson*, *spokesperson*, etc., are reserved for women, the implication—conscious or otherwise—is that *woman* is a taboo word for which a euphemism must be substituted:

> "The Planning and Zoning Commission and the Board of Education last week elected new chairpersons. . . . James Doe, newly elected Planning and Zoning member . . . will serve as chairman. . . . Catherine Roe will serve as chairperson of the Board of Education. . . ."

This lopsided usage may also subtly derogate the woman referred to, as when a headline calling Golda Meir an "Elder Statesperson" appeared in a newspaper that allows neither *chairperson* nor *spokesperson* in its pages.

One pluralization of *person* is *people*. This is a common and natural usage, despite the frequently cited "rule" that *persons* is the correct form to use when referring to an exact or relatively small number of people. One would not say, for example,

> We're inviting a few persons over for supper

or

> Our church adopted eight Vietnamese boat persons.

Similarly, most compound words ending in *person* sound more natural when pluralized with *people:*

> Jewelry by three local craftspeople is displayed in the bank window.

> We have seventeen salespeople covering the north central states.

> According to their spokespeople, none of the candidates will campaign on Yom Kippur.

If *chairperson* survives intact, *chairpeople* may prove to be the natural and most acceptable plural.

The increased recognition being accorded *person* has led to the emergence of *personhood,* a word so new that few dictionaries even list it. Now that *personhood* has become part of the lexicon, it is hard to see how English was able to get along without it. For example, neither *manhood* nor *womanhood* would have expressed the meaning Congresswoman Barbara Jordan intended when, supporting extension of the ratification deadline for the Equal Rights Amendment, she asked in 1978,

> "Who am I to say we should short-circuit the time to seek personhood in society?"

Nor in the following statement could one substitute *womanhood* for *personhood:*

> "[Rape] is experienced by women as a total assault on their personhood. . . ."

Suffragist, Suffragette

A resolution supporting suffrage for women was first presented to the British Parliament in 1851, but for more than half a century neither the government nor the press paid much attention to the cause, its leaders, or the growing numbers of women and men in British suffrage societies. In 1903 Emmeline Pankhurst and her daughters, Christabel and Sylvia, formed the Women's Social and Political Union (WSPU) with the aim of publicizing their demand for enfranchisement by heckling politicians at meetings and by demonstrations and acts of civil disobedience.

The technique worked. The activities of the militant suffragists were soon being reported regularly by British newspapers, often—to be sure—with scorn or amused condescension, but the WSPU leaders believed that any attention was better than none. One paper referred to the militants as "martyrettes," and in 1906 the *Daily Mail* coined the term *suffragette,* which the WSPU immediately adopted, hardening the "g." As Christabel Pankhurst later wrote, "Just 'want the vote' was the notion conveyed by the older appellation [but] as a famous anecdote had it, 'the Suffragettes, they mean to get it.' "

Not all militant British suffragists were enthusiastic about the name, however. A comment by the historian Trevor Lloyd is revealing: "[T]he supporters of the Suffrage Societies were known as Suffragists, so *it was natural* to call their more violent allies in the WSPU 'Suffragettes.' " (Italics added.) Since the *-ette* ending in English also signals either small size or imitation, attaching it to the "more violent allies" could only be considered "natural" as an uneasy effort to discount them. Lloyd (writing in 1971) adds that "by now almost everyone who supported votes for women in the days before the First World War is liable to be called a suffragette. But at the time the suffragettes were a very special group—they did not always like the nickname, and sometimes called themselves 'militants'—with a special approach to politics."

Women in the United States who from 1848 to 1920 worked to get the vote for women—including Elizabeth Cady Stanton, Lucretia Mott, Susan B. Anthony, Lucy Stone, Ida B. Wells, Anna Howard Shaw, Mary Church Terrell, Carrie Chapman Catt, and Alice Paul—called themselves "suffragists." To call them "suffragettes" is historically inaccurate and, since none of these women chose to adopt that belittling term as their British sisters had done, it is also inadvertently demeaning.

Tomboy

The implication of the word *tomboy* is that an active, inquisitive, energetic girl acts like a boy, not a girl. In other words, she is abnormal for one of her sex.

Seldom is the socialization of children reflected more directly in language than in this term, although the word *sissy* comes close, especially when applied to a boy. Perhaps the chief difference in the effect of the two words is that *sissy*, which comes from *sister* (just as *buddy* comes from *brother*), is an overt insult whereas *tomboy* purports to be a compliment. In the first instance the child's answer can be clear and self-enhancing: "I'm *not* a sissy!" In the second, neither denial nor assent is appropriate.

Although English lacks sex-specific words to describe the kind of girl who is labeled a "tomboy," it does have an abundance of sex-neutral terms to choose from. Words like *strong, vigorous, direct, adventurous, spirited, self-confident, competitive,* and *physically courageous* can serve the same purpose without confusing the child's self-perception and sense of sexual identity.

Women's Liberation

People who use the term *women's lib* probably would not dream of saying "black lib" or "lib for Native Americans," and they may not realize what this offhand treatment of a serious subject reveals about their attitudes. Abbreviations like *black lib, women's lib,* and *fem lib* are apt to be the hallmark of either hostile or shallow thinking.

The social movement to achieve rights and opportunities for women equal to those of men, whether one agrees with it or not, is a historic fact. When its goals are achieved, the terms *feminism, women's movement,* and *women's liberation* will be of historic interest only.

Reference Notes

In addition to the specific references cited in these notes, we found the following papers of particular interest and would like to acknowledge their contributions to our thinking:

Nancy M. Henley, "This New Species That Seeks a New Language: On Sexism in Language and Language Change," paper presented at the Conference on Language and Gender, University of California at Santa Cruz, May 4, 1979.

Patricia C. Nichols, "Planning for Language Change," paper presented at the Modern Language Association of America Forum on Women and Language, New York, December 27–30, 1978.

Maija S. Blaubergs, "Sociolinguistic Change Towards Nonsexist Language: An Overview and Analysis of Misunderstandings and Misapplications," paper presented at the Ninth World Congress of Sociology, Uppsala, Sweden, August 1978.

Introduction

Page 6 The Chisholm quotation is from Shirley Chisholm, "The 51% Minority," in *The American Sisterhood: Writings of the Feminist Movement from Colonial Times to the Present,* Wendy Martin, ed., New York, Harper & Row, 1972.

Chapter 1

Page 10 Among studies which report and discuss evidence indicating that the so-called generics *man* and *men* (and compounds incorporating them) are not generally understood to include females are the following:

Johanna S. DeStefano, Mary W. Kuhner, and Harold B. Pepinsky, "An Investigation of Referents of Selected Sex-Indefinite Terms in English," paper presented at the Ninth World Congress of Sociology, Uppsala, Sweden, August 1978.

LaVisa Cam Wilson, "Teachers' Inclusion of Males and Females in Generic Nouns," *Research in the Teaching of English,* May 1978, Vol. 12, No. 2, pp. 155–161.

Ozella M. Y. Eberhart, "Elementary Students' Understanding of Certain Masculine and Neutral Generic Nouns," doctoral dissertation, Kansas State University,. 1976, *Dissertation Abstracts,* 1976, Vol. 37, pp. 4113A–4114A. (University Microfilms No. 76–29,993.)

Linda Harrison, "Cro-Magnon Woman—In Eclipse," *The Science Teacher,* April 1975, pp. 8–11.

Linda Harrison and Richard Passero, "Sexism in the Language of Elementary School Textbooks," *Science and Children,* January 1975, Vol. 12, pp. 22–25.

Joseph W. Schneider and Sally L. Hacker, "Sex Role Imagery and the Use of the Generic 'Man' in Introductory Texts: A Case in the Sociology of Sociology," *The American Sociologist,* February 1973, Vol. 8, No. 1, pp. 12–18.

For an analysis of the cognitive exclusion of women in common "generic" uses of *man,* see Julia P. Stanley, "Gender-Marking in American English: Usage and Reference," in Alleen Pace Nilsen, Haig Bosmajian, H. Lee Gershuny, and Julia P. Stanley, *Sexism and Language,* Urbana, Ill., National Council of Teachers of English, 1977.

An interesting discussion of the "reasonable man" doctrine in law and its nonapplicability to women is provided by Ronald K. L. Collins in "Language, History and the Legal Process: A Profile of the 'Reasonable Man,'" *Rutgers-Camden Law Journal,* Winter 1977, Vol. 8, No. 2, pp. 311–323.

Page 27 "Were our State a pure democracy . . ." is from a letter to Samuel Kerchval dated September 5, 1816, reprinted in *The Works of Thomas Jefferson,* Paul Leicester Ford, editor, New York, G. P. Putnam's Sons, 1905, Federal Edition, Vol. 12, pp. 15–16.

Page 29 The effect of sex-labeled job titles on students' perceptions of career options was studied by Sandra and Daryl Bem and reported in their article "Does Sex-Biased Job Advertising 'Aid and Abet' Sex Discrimination?" *Journal of Applied Social Psy-*

chology, January–March 1973, Vol. 3, No. 1, pp. 6–18. A similar study was conducted by N. Shepelak, D. Ogden, and D. Tobin at Indiana University. A brief description of the results appears in Norma J. Shepelak, "Neanderthal Person Revisited," *The American Sociologist,* May 1976, Vol. 11, No. 2, pp. 90–92.

Chapter 2

Page 35 The historical background on "generic" *he* is drawn primarily from two sources: Ann Bodine, "Androcentrism in Prescriptive Grammar: Singular 'They,' Sex-Indefinite 'He,' and 'He or She,' " *Language in Society,* August 1975, Vol. 4, No. 2, pp. 129–145; and Julia P. Stanley, "Sexist Grammar," *College English,* March 1978, Vol. 39, No. 7, pp. 800–811.

Page 37 Reports of studies confirming the failure of "generic" *he* to represent both sexes adequately include the following:

Donald G. McKay, "Prescriptive Grammar and the Pronoun Problem," in Nancy Henley, Barrie Thorne, and Cheris Kramarae, *Language and Sex II,* Rowley, Mass., Newbury House Publishers, Inc., Fall 1980.

Jeanette Silveira, "Generic Masculine Words and Thinking," *Women's Studies International Quarterly,* 1980, Vol. 3, Nos. 2 and 3.

Janice Moulton, George M. Robinson, and Cherin Elias, "Sex Bias in Language Use: 'Neutral' Pronouns That Aren't," *American Psychologist,* November 1978, Vol. 33, No. 11, pp. 1032–1036.

DeStefano, Kuhner, and Pepinsky, "An Investigation of Referents of Selected Sex-Indefinite Terms in English," cited above.

Wendy Martyna, "What Does 'He' Mean? Use of the Generic Masculine," *Journal of Communication,* Winter 1978, Vol. 28, No. 1, pp. 131–138.

Barbara Bate, "Nonsexist Language Use in Transition," *Journal of Communication,* Winter 1978, Vol. 28, No. 1, pp. 139–149.

Virginia Kidd, "A Study of the Images Produced Through the Use of the Male Pronoun as the Generic," *Moments in Contemporary Rhetoric and Communication,* 1971, Vol. 1, No. 2, pp. 25–30.

Page 46 A review of recently proposed common-gender pronouns and examples of their use in published materials appears in Casey Miller and Kate Swift, *Words and Women,* Garden City, N.Y., Anchor Press/Doubleday and Co., 1977, pp. 116–118.

Experiments testing the effectiveness of various proposed sex-inclusive pronouns are being conducted by Donald G. MacKay and his colleagues in the Department of Psychology, University of California at Los Angeles.

Chapter 3

Page 51 The information on Third World farmers is from John J. Gilligan, "Women and Their Importance to the Third World," *The Washington Post,* June 24, 1978.

Page 63 The Poole quotation appears in Bodine, "Androcentrism in Prescriptive Grammar," cited above. The Murray quotation appears in Stanley, "Sexist Grammar," also cited above.

Chapter 4

Page 70 A discerning discussion of the terms that mental health professionals use in referring to female patients is provided by Harriet E. Lerner, "Girls, Ladies, or Women? The Unconscious Dynamics of Language Choice," *Comprehensive Psychiatry,* March/April 1976, Vol. 17, No. 2, pp. 295–299.

Page 77 The psycholinguist Ethel Strainchamps postulates another reason that speakers of English avoid *woman:* it phonetically symbolizes small size and low status. Strainchamps's discoveries about the gender system of English, in which sounds reflect consensus not only on size and shape but on status and sex associations, are discussed in Miller and Swift, *Words and Women,* cited above, p. 162.

Page 78 We wish to thank Marjorie Vogel of Pittsburgh, Pennsylvania, for sharing with us her insights on the language used to describe the work women and men do at home.

Page 80 The eight-part series of articles entitled "Women at Work" appeared in the *Wall Street Journal* between August 28 and September 22, 1978.

Chapter 5

Page 95 The Wilson quotation appears in Bodine, "Androcentrism in Prescriptive Grammar," cited above.

Page 101 We wish to thank Jane Mollman, who also likes to be referred to as Mrs. J. Peter Mollman, for allowing us to use her poem "In typing *Ms.* for *Mrs.*"

Chapter 6

Page 106 The inclusion of both the masculine- and feminine-gender forms of personal nouns and pronouns in the Latin of Roman law is discussed, with examples, by Otto Jespersen in *Language: Its Nature, Development and Origin*, New York, Henry Holt and Company, 1922, pp. 347–348.

Page 117 The account of the discovery of digitalis, including the Withering quotation, is from Margaret B. Kreig, *Green Medicine: The Search for Plants That Heal*, Chicago, Rand McNally & Company, 1964, pp. 207–214.

Page 120 The Pankhurst quotation is from Christabel Pankhurst, *Unshackled: The Story of How We Won the Vote*, ed. by the Rt. Hon. Lord Pethick-Lawrence of Peasdale, London, Hutchison, 1959, pp. 62–63. The Lloyd quotation is from Trevor Lloyd, *Suffragettes International: The World-Wide Campaign for Women's Rights*, New York, American Heritage Press, and London, Macdonald Unit 75, 1971, p. 49.

Index